CHRISTOPHER M. LANGAN

FAQs About Reality

Chris Langan's Social Media Posts

Book One

Quora

Mega Foundation Press

www.ctmu.org

www.patreon.com/CTMU

First Paperback Edition

Published by
Mega Foundation Press, Inc.
Princeton, MO

info@megapress.org

Typeset in Roboto
by Michał Szczęsny

Langan, C. M. (Christopher Michael)
FAQs About Reality: Chris Langan's Social Media Posts
1. Metaphysics 2. General Knowledge
ISBN 978-0-9719162-3-4

FAQs About Reality

Chris Langan's
Social Media Posts

Book One: Quora

To the Members of the CTMU Community
who faithfully follow my work

CONTENTS

T

W

Publisher's Note

"FAQs About Reality" contains Chris Langan's answers to questions posted on Quora during the years he was active, 2016-2019. Langan was banned from Quora for his conservative worldview and uncompromising debate style. Although Langan never broke Quora's rules or violated its terms of service, he was summarily deplatformed without warning. All of his posts were deleted or orphaned. With the help of members of the Mega Foundation and CTMU Community, the majority of his work on Quora was preserved in this volume.

ACADEMIA

Academic admission

1.   Is there a "back door" to top universities?

Absolutely not, unless you have personal connections who can wire you into the system (or a fashionable complexion or sexual orientation which "merits" an exception).

I happen to be in a position to know this for a fact. I've been featured in a NY Times number 1 best-seller as someone who fell through the cracks of the education system, but was nevertheless intellectually well-suited for a faculty position at a top institution like Harvard. Naturally, Harvard ignored this suggestion (apparently, Larry Summers – or should that be Drew Gilpin Faust – was too busy to notice the book and/or too important to care). I was subsequently contacted by a student at Syracuse who thought I should be welcomed onto the faculty; no cigar. Other similar initiatives failed as well.

Prior to that, my wife – who happens to have a very respectable PhD – had scoured academia for PhD programs willing to admit students directly, regardless of prior credentials. She found just a couple, albeit not in the US: they were located in Wales and South Africa. Neither wanted me even as a grad student, despite my evident ability to intellectually annihilate most members of their respective faculties in their chosen disciplines. Finally, we were forced to realize that it was all a facade – at best, these places had merely established a pretext for admitting supposed "outsiders" through their nepotistic, crony-based, insiders-only friends-and-relatives programs. It was a complete joke.

In case this series of unfortunate events seems vanishingly improbable, consider what academia is actually about these days. First, it comprises a diffuse multinational metacorporation which is unabashedly in business for profit. Tuition, government grants, research funding, sports income, endowments, investments – everything with monetary value feeds the bottom line, and this is ultimately all that counts. Secondly, its educational mandate has steadily given way to a mandate for ideological standardization, indoctrination, and socialization, putting it in the business of psychological mass production and social engineering. Unless one appears receptive to its standardized psychological conditioning, one's personal qualifications are all but irrelevant to admission. Thirdly, academia is an intellectual trade union which, while admirably inclusive when the money and credit flow inward, turns highly exclusive when the money threatens to flow outward. Defy it or even try to jump the queue, and unless you're one of the chosen few, it will make an example of you. Best get it straight as quickly as possible: in Academia, Inc., it's strictly pay to play.

But despair ye not, for there is still the conventional route to academic certification: run the admissions gauntlet, sit there like a good little boy or girl for 4–8 years or so, soak up the ignorance and opinionation of your instructors while latching onto any crumbs of actual knowledge that may accidentally exit their mouths as they scramble to advance their academic careers, and incur the customary mountain of debt. Then maybe, *just maybe*, you'll be grudgingly admitted to the club.

(Alas, I no longer have that kind of spare time on my hands. How lucky for me that I can nevertheless make nattering monkeys out of most professional academics, and refrain from doing so more often only because it feels like taking candy from babies. ;)

January 17, 2018

Academic credentials

2.   Is it true that "anyone with the slightest experience with academia would laugh at the very notion of some journal editor even looking at a submission from someone without academic credentials, even if that person really was an Einstein"?

Over the years, I've asked roughly the same question of many academics on a more or less casual basis. The answers fell into two categories which may be illustrated as follows:

(A) "Unsolicited papers may be submitted to most academic journals without any mention of credentials and are usually subjected to blind review. Most of the time, the editor and reviewers either know or can figure out with whom they're dealing, and have an incentive to obtain such information insofar as their own reputations are riding on the papers that they accept. In any case, a few papers have indeed been accepted from unknown and uncredentialed people over the years. My advice would be to first submit two or three papers that are more or less obvious and clear-cut – just this side of trivial, but with a little something of merit to perk up their ears – and only then one's more profound work, which might still be rejected. You might also try convincing a known academic to co-author with you – of course, he or she will probably want first-author credit, so that's something to bear in mind."

(B) "If you're the least bit out of the mainstream, don't bother. 99.9 percent of the time, journal editors know exactly with whom they're dealing, and if you're an unknown with anything important to say, they'll find out about you with some browsing and a couple of phone calls. For a journal editor, the down side of accepting bad work greatly outweighs the up side of accepting passable work, so your identity and credentials will be looked into, and you'll never get the benefit of the doubt. Because most work by uncredentialed unknowns is deficient, the assumption *will* immediately be that your work isn't worth anything; on the other hand, any good ideas in your paper can be misappropriated by your 'blind reviewers' with complete impunity, and as an unknown, you won't be able to get a word in edgewise. My advice is this: pay your quarter or half-million dollars for an advanced degree from a top institution, make a few friends in the field, and then try your luck – you'll get much better results."

So unfortunately, barring exceptional circumstances and solid connections in one's field, the answer would seem to be that yes, the vast majority of academic journal editors do *not* seriously consider submissions from authors without academic credentials. This is especially likely for potentially dangerous or disruptive work that approaches the originality and importance of Einstein's, especially if it is hard to understand or more than a little interdisciplinary (most academics are too busy to spend much time trying to understand what they don't already know, and too specialized to sign off on interdisciplinary content).

Unexceptional papers by unknown authors have a slight but definite advantage over more profound papers, which are nearly certain to be rejected due to the author's low perceived status or "lack of standing in the field". If one's name happens to be publicly known, and one has been subjected to trolling or half-baked amateur criticism which makes one seem "controversial" (as might have been the case with Einstein had the Internet existed in his day), one might as well forget about it – even sterling academic credentials might not have helped.

Here's a similar response that I gave to an interviewer a few years back:

> The academic world is far too wrapped up in itself to make time for anything or anybody else. The situation is exacerbated by a tendency among academics to assume that if it wasn't coughed up from the belly of the academic beast, it can't be worth a glance. The prospects are especially dim for potentially game-changing work that is perceived to run afoul of academic orthodoxy, threaten the economic status quo, or have difficult social or political ramifications.

> As I've already mentioned, academia has all but monopolized gainful intellectual activity through its stranglehold on intellectual certification. The dependence of economic opportunity on academic certification is impossible to miss; it should be no less obvious that this dependency relationship extends to the intellectual advancement of mankind. Woe to any would-be contributor who parts ways with the academic machine, for intellectual commerce is governed by a publish-or-perish economy of publication and citation in academic journals, wherein the obstacles to publication and proper attribution are proportional to the obscurity of the author, the importance and controversiality of the topic, and the level and prominence of the periodical. As a

result, important technical works by authors without academic credentials and affiliations are unlikely to be published or cited, and even if these authors beat the odds against them, they cannot benefit in any meaningful way from their effort.

There are at least two obvious reasons for this situation.

(1) Much like an intellectual trade union, academia reserves all of its benefits for members, affording nonmembers no standing, no incentives, and no avenue of recourse should others use their ideas without credit. By making sure that people cannot get along without academic credentials, academia assures itself of a continued influx of paying clients and thus feeds its pyramidal growth economy without necessarily delivering all of the educational services it owes the public.

(2) Professional academics consider it risky to associate with those who may be perceived as "unqualified", preferring to cite well-credentialed, well-connected authors likely to reflect well on their academic reputations. This aversion to risk applies a fortiori to journal editors and reviewers, and even to the commercial publishing houses specializing in scholarly nonfiction. This greatly increases the likelihood that meaningful contributions by academic outsiders will not be published, and if they are, that they will be used without credit.

Unfortunately, this means that people without academic credentials have nothing to gain, but everything to lose, by attempting to publish in academic journals, and thus that academic journals do not qualify as a rational venue for their ideas. Just as one need not step off a succession of cliffs to understand what will happen if one steps off the next cliff, one need not repeatedly hurl oneself at the closed shop door of academia to know that one will simply bounce off, the sound of impact echoing without citation or appreciation if at all.

March 30, 2018

Academic indoctrination

3.   What would be your advice for highly intelligent youth who have lost academic motivation as a result of being unchallenged?

First, let me say that I sympathize with what would appear to be the motives behind this kind of question, which no professional educator is in a position to answer honestly. But that being understood, you should probably resign yourself to the following facts:

(1) The main purpose of modern education is not to prepare you for life as a scholar. In fact, it is not for worthwhile education of any kind. It is for indoctrination, socialization, and classifying you as either (a) a good little drone who can be put to work and squeezed interminably for revenue by your "betters" in the power structure, or (b) someone who should be marginalized and economically disenfranchised *en route* to possible incarceration by the penal system, at which point your "betters" will have their way with you anyway. All pretensions to the contrary exist strictly in furtherance of this goal. You may find a few instructors who delude themselves about this and actually try to help their students learn, but this is no longer the norm.

(2) Intelligence has been completely replaced by academic credentials as an employment criterion. You do not inhabit a meritocracy; the world you inhabit is run by only moderately intelligent, mostly filthy-rich sociopaths who place no value on truth or knowledge for the betterment of mankind or for their own sake. Thus, your prospects of social and economic advancement are not enhanced by extraordinary intelligence. They have far more to do with your credentials, your connections, and sadly enough, your complexion (the more non-White you are, the better you can avail yourself of affirmative action, take employment from better-qualified people, and avoid termination due to any bad attitude you may exhibit in negative appreciation for the affirmative action you received). Remember, capitalizing on one's intelligence requires material resources, and if those resources are denied you, your intelligence will not help you.

(3) If you flounder, do not expect your teachers to help you unless you have the proper complexion for it. If you are nonwhite and thus fashionably complexioned, educators can get bureaucratic brownie points by treating your mind as "a terrible thing to waste"; bending over backwards to help you makes them look good to their superiors in the bureaucracy.

But if you are White, then you are highly likely to be deemed (a) automatically guilty of "White privilege", (b) an undeserving beneficiary of US colonialism who needs to be punished for the unspeakable effrontery of your existence to the rest of mankind, and (c) justly destined for demographic genocide as "more deserving" immigrants from overpopulated Third World cesspools, transported here using what little money you may have succeeded in accumulating, rightfully displace you from your ancestral homeland and the human gene pool.

(4) If you are rejected by the "education" system for any reason, you become ineligible for participation in the modern economy. Without connections, you probably won't be able to find work as anything more than a janitor (if that), and your life will be rendered economically worthless. It is the possible avoidance of this plight for which you are paying when you buy a college "education". It used to be that a college education was a virtual guarantee of decent employment; this is no longer true, at least for White people. It is only the fear of complete, permanent economic exclusion that induces modern students to pay up to 20 (twenty) times for academic credentials what they cost in the 1970's (that extra money is being stuffed in the pockets of an ever-expanding pool of corporate-administrative yuppies, by the way – think of an insatiable army of Larry Summers clones). As soon as you are rejected by the education system, you effectively become ineligible for gainful employment; you probably won't be able to find a decent job of any kind, and your life will be rendered economically worthless as a result. I'm sure you can imagine the attending hardships.

(5) In a totally materialistic society, intelligence is of value only when it is turned to exclusively material pursuits ... that is, to the acquisition of money and what it buys. Your worth as an individual is measured strictly by the amount of money your socio-economic betters think they can make from you, or in rare cases, the amount of public credit they think they can get for helping you. Yes, you may be allowed to console yourself with feel-good platitudes like "money isn't everything" and "the best things in life are free"; talk, as they say, is cheap. But let's face it, you won't have much time for idealistic soliloquies as you scramble, against all the odds, to survive.

Incidentally, I haven't just rendered an opinion here out of prejudice; I've been invited to answer this question for a reason – i.e., because of who and what I am – and am merely explaining what I've learned from my own life experiences. That is, encouraged by the fact that I've never

7

met a college professor I couldn't crush intellectually like an aluminum beer can, I went the hard way and did what I felt called to do in spite of everything you've just read. Given the will to do the same, you can succeed on your own terms even after being thrown away by the venal and corrupt indoctrination apparatus that passes for an education system in this country. You'll probably remain poor, unfortunately, but forewarned is forearmed.

Doubt any or all of this if you like, but don't say that no one tried to set you straight. It's simply not what many of us think it is out there, and the sooner you realize it, the better off you'll probably be.

December 26, 2017

4.   Does Chris Langan realize that his brash, impertinent rants against academics are likely contributing to his theory not being taken seriously by many people who have heard of him?

Yes, I realize that openly criticizing academia is likely to precipitate a certain insufferable subset of academics and academic administrators into a permanent sulk. But I doubt that anything is lost by it, as at this point, I have ample reason to think that I'd never have gotten a fair shake from that crowd anyway. Accordingly, when people ask questions about academia and I choose to answer them, I'll continue to do so honestly.

Secondly, I don't "rant" against academia *as it should be*; I deplore *what it has b+-ecome* in spite of the best intentions of its progenitors. Academia, having turned away from its educational mandate to pursue alternative missions including disinformative mass indoctrination, social engineering, shameless profiteering, and pandering like $20 hookers to the military-industrial-security complex and the purveyors of identity politics, is currently destroying Western Civilization, an institution that is far greater than academia and which must be preserved for the sake of mankind. Criticism, and more if necessary, is therefore exactly what academia needs.

Thirdly, I was ranted at, and against – often behind my back, I later learned – by academics at times in my life when it could (and did) hurt me the most, which of course had the cumulative effect of permanently depriving academia of any immunity from criticism that I may previously have granted it. Academia employs an embarrassingly large percentage of mean, nasty, sneaky people of Machiavellian bent, who thrive by positioning themselves advantageously in bureaucratic webs and anonymously pulling strands to the detriment of their chosen enemies. Not good at all, especially when they target those with important contributions of which they are themselves collectively incapable.

It's like this. If you're an organizational pickpocket, and you get caught lifting someone's wallet, and you really want forgiveness, you don't blame the victim. You suck it up, admit what you did, own up to your moral flaws, give back the wallet, and promise to do better. Why does everyone seem to assume that academia is above any need to do the same? Think about it a little.

[**Note**: This question closely resembles one which was erased by the questioner after I had already responded to it, and after my response had received well over 20 upvotes in the course of two hours this morning. For future reference, I don't appreciate having my written material destroyed by indignant trolls after their trolling backfires on them – if you want to be a smart ass, learn how to take your lumps. Thanks for your attention.]

December 29, 2017

Academic jacket

5.   What is it like to be fired as a PhD student for not performing well?

One of the most-viewed answers to this question includes the sentence "The University is actually a rather forgiving institution." This may be true on some occasions, but a qualification is in order: as a rule, the university will treat you "forgivingly" only in proportion to the amount of money, prestige, and approval you can bring it. If it sees no prospect of gain from you, and if you can't even help fill an ethnic quota for it, then once something too pejorative goes into your "jacket", your academic career is quite likely to be over.

In case the meaning of "jacket" is unclear, most of us know that grade school and high school teachers everywhere are fond of threatening problem students with critical notations on their "permanent records". "Jacket" is synonymous with "permanent record". This general phenomenon is not confined to academia; for example, those who are sent to prison quickly learn that there is a "jacket" which follows (or more accurately, precedes) them as they make their ways through the penal system.

9

Even when they are moved from one prison to another, its contents determine how they are treated. **As it is for convicts, so it is for students**.

One almost never sees the contents of one's own jacket. Consequently, even if it is packed with sheer libel motivated by the personal animosity and venom of those with access to it, no one but its subject is ever held to account for it. It typically emerges from its locked file cabinet only when being secretly updated or reviewed by parole boards or academic star chambers. Once a vindictive academic bureaucrat has gotten into a snit over one's "bad attitude" and written something awful in it – and academia notoriously teems with vindictive backstabbers who thrive and proliferate under layers of bureaucratic secrecy – one might as well call it a day (or, given the dire economic cost of not having academic credentials, a life).

In this unfortunate event, academia expects one to blame everything on oneself. "Oh woe is me!" one is expected to wail. "I screwed up! My folly knew no bounds!" And indeed, the student sometimes bears a large measure of responsibility for his/her own failure. But sometimes, grave injustices are done by academic miscreants who, while remaining safely hidden in the shadows, snicker into their palms with sadistic glee at the pain they have succeeded in causing. The more personal interaction a student must have with professional academics, the greater the risk. The risk becomes higher than ever in graduate school, where the wrong word to some professorial intellectual narcissist could spell total disaster.

We all know that academia likes to portray itself as spotless and above reproach; this is only natural given its need to justify its accelerating consumption of societal resources. But sadly, this image is increasingly undeserved. When it comes down to the nitty-gritty, academia is exactly what it appears to be: a venal bureaucratic rat's nest seething with petty rivalry, intellectual jealousy, Machiavellian intrigue, and internecine political conflict. At this point, no one should make the mistake of assuming that those who have found their callings within it are immune to its rot, and no one who finds oneself on the wrong side of it should rush to blame it all on oneself.

January 24, 2017

Academic reception

6. Is Chris Langan probably the greatest philosopher and mathematician of all time?

Let's just put it like this: if my work were understood in academia, which jealously controls the distribution of credit for advanced intellectual productions and has at its disposal a vast army of enforcers including proud certificants, adoring groupies, and Internet trolls who all suffer from something like the Stockholm syndrome and therefore treat it as their Mother Church, some people would probably be making some very positive statements along those lines.

However, in addition to having parted ways with academia, I suffer from two related problems: (1) many people evidently cannot understand what I write about the CTMU, and (2) instead of blaming any part of this on themselves, they blame it entirely on me. These problems can be expressed a bit more formally as, respectively, the Hollingworth "30 point rule" and the Dunning-Kruger effect. The former says that even people who are measurably smarter than average will find it hard or impossible to share their deeper thoughts with those whose IQ's are more than about two standard deviations lower, and the latter says that less intelligent people tend to overrate their own intelligence relative to that of more intelligent people.

Both of these problems have been vastly amplified by decades of intensive social engineering designed to shift the intellectual bell curve objectively downward while shifting the subjective intellectual self-regard of the majority upward. The main tool of the social engineers is the indoctrination engine of Academia, Inc., an engine so efficient that it is in fact self-indoctrinating; its members actually believe the orthodoxies and political doctrine they dispense. Academia constitutes a pyramidal growth economy which has now passed the saturation point, but quite possibly has entered its decline too late to do society any good.

Obviously, as academia has contrived to establish a near-monopoly on advance certification for any form of employment more desirable than ditch-digger and toilet-cleaner, academic rejection costs people like me dearly. However, although I was initially willing to take some of the responsibility for my style of expression and lack of formal education, I have since learned in a variety of ways that this was never actually justified. That is, I've been forced to conclude that the nonrecognition of me and my work is academia's fault, academia's responsibility, and academia's future problem. (We could add "atheistic trolls" to the mix, but this should be enough on which to chew for now.)

I hope this helps clear things up a little.

July 26, 2018

Tuition inflation

7.   You are given 20 million dollars up front in cash, or you are given access to higher education of any sort for life. What would be your choice?

Take the twenty and spend it quick. Tuition inflation guaranties that in 10–15 years, $20 million won't be enough to pry any self-respecting corporate administrator of Academia, Inc. out of his diamond-encrusted gold-and-ebony faculty-powered litter, and the deal would be broken. Plan ahead, for Pete's sake!

February 04, 2017

AFTERLIFE

Possible outcomes

8. How many kinds of after-life existences are there? Or do we simply merge with God and have our soul/personality dissipate into one consciousness?

On the most basic level, just two: one's soul, or connection to God, is intact (good news), or it is corrupt and the connection is severed (bad news).

Without a soul that is at least partially intact, embedment in God cannot be maintained, and one is cut off from the source of existence. In this case, "the afterlife" consists of the disintegration, reduction, and recycling of personal identity, which is desperately resisted and thus a source of unimaginable despair (some call it "hell"). On the other hand, if the soul remains intact, the identity can persist in any of a number of specific ways depending on its strength and configuration.

Due to the possibility of a negative "life-after-death" outcome, this may not be the most popular answer you receive for this question. However, it is the *real* answer with a real basis in metaphysical logic.

May 15, 2017

ATHEISM

Atheism or agnosticism

9.   How is atheism different from agnosticism?

An "agnostic atheist" is merely an agnostic, unless someone can explain how one differs from the other.

A case can be made that atheism has two definitions, because it can be broken down into lexical constituents in two ways: (1) *athe(o)+ism* (belief in the nonexistence of God) and (2) *a+theism* (nonbelief in the existence of God). As an atheist, one can be either 1 and 2 (1 implies 2), or just 2. "Agnostic atheists" seem to have chosen 2 alone.

Here's their problem: if one chooses definition 2 alone, this implies that one is not described by definition 1, which makes one an agnostic plain and simple (one believes in neither the existence nor the nonexistence of God). Only if one subscribes to both definitions 1 and 2 is one a real atheist. Take your pick.

Quora has many people claiming to be "agnostic atheists". It almost looks like none of them have thought it through as anything but a rather sneaky way to swell the ranks of atheism by reclassifying agnostics as atheists with a trick of etymology. Unless, of course, some "agnostic atheist" can satisfactorily explain the nomenclature.

I suspect that some might explain it as follows: "An agnostic atheist is one who believes that *there exists no evidence* for the existence of God" (an epistemological rather than an ontological claim). But aside from the fact that this has never been shown, many agnostics believe it as well, so again there is no real distinction; every "agnostic atheist" can be more economically described as an agnostic.

In other words, the ruse has failed.

June 26, 2017

14

10.   Do atheists solely rely on logic?

There can be little doubt that atheists, as diverse as they may be, often seem to *think* that they "rely on logic". Many appear to pride them-selves on it.

However, when one closely examines their arguments, it often turns out that their ideas of logic leave something to be desired. For example, according to the kind of "logic" on which many of them depend, there is no difference between an agnostic and the kind of "atheist" calling himself an "agnostic atheist".

To wit, agnostics and "agnostic atheists" both answer NO to both of the following questions:

(1) "Do you believe in the *existence* of God?"

(2) "Do you believe in the *nonexistence* of God?"

Previously, a real atheist was conventionally defined as someone who answers NO to the first question and YES to the second. This is quite a change!

The idea behind this semantic switcheroo seems to be that an "agnostic atheist" who denies that he actively believes in the nonexistence of God has no burden of proof. But clearly, a self-styled "atheist" who does not actively believe in the nonexistence of God is just another agnostic!

Obviously, a group which has trouble properly distinguishing itself from another group with which it has historically been contrasted may not be the best group on which to rely for a definition of "logic".

June 10, 2018

11.   What is the evidence in support of atheism?

There are two definitions of atheism. It can mean either (1) the belief that God does not exist [*athe(o)* + *ism*], or (2) a lack of belief in the existence of God [*a* + *theism*, which, when accompanied by a lack of belief in the nonexistence of God, is identical to agnosticism]. There is no evidence for atheism under either definition.

Bear in mind that in light of the law of excluded middle, those "atheists" who are simply agnostic are merely begging the question; they cannot maintain their position indefinitely unless there is no evidence either for or against the existence of God ... but there is no evidence that this is the case. In fact, there may be evidence that God exists, e.g., the existence of reality itself, with which God may coincide in whole or in part. So unlike atheism (1), atheism (2) is not really a definite theological position.

Note that many of the self-styled "atheists" answering this question are merely agnostics who falsely believe that they have permanent grounds for their lack of belief. The proper question to ask such an "atheist" is this: "What is your evidence that the existence of God cannot be proven?" An "atheist" who cannot provide such evidence might as well get off the bandwagon, admit that he doesn't really know anything of theological import, and call himself an "agnostic".

June 17, 2017

Belief

12.   Is atheism a betlief or a conclusion?

Atheism is definitely a belief.

The word *atheism* can be broken down into lexical constituents in two ways: (1) *athe(o)* + *ism* (belief in the nonexistence of God) and (2) *a* + *theism* (nonbelief in the existence of God). An atheist must conform to both definitions (1 implies 2), not just definition 2.

Why? If one chooses definition 2 alone, this implies that one is not described by definition 1, which makes one an *agnostic* as conventionally defined in juxtaposition to theism and atheism. That is, lacking knowledge supporting either the existence or the nonexistence of God, one believes in neither.

Many atheists, some calling themselves "agnostic atheists", have taken to claiming that they are covered by definition 2 alone. Why? Because it seems to excuse them from any burden of proof. However, this renders their position theologically indefinite and therefore irrelevant. They merely lack belief in God *without having any good reason* for not believing in God, and thus have no definite theological position. (If one has a good reason for not believing in the existence of God, then one conforms to definition 1 after all.) Only if one subscribes to both definitions 1 and 2 is one a real atheist.

Any atheist who responds by saying that his "good reason" for not believing in God is that "there is no evidence for the existence of God" merely incurs another burden of proof, this one epistemological: he needs to *prove* (or at least confirm) that there is no evidence for the existence of God. But as no atheist is in a position to attest to anything but his own subjective knowledge state regarding such matters, this is out of the question.

So the bottom line is that if you want to call yourself an atheist, then you must believe in the nonexistence of God, period ... and once again, you have a burden of proof to that effect. Otherwise, you're just a garden variety agnostic, and in that case, you shouldn't be butting into theological discussions as though you have anything definite to say. Nor should you be claiming the rational high ground without rational justification of your own.

As for atheism being a "conclusion", that depends on how it is inferred and from what premises. Unfortunately, the best theoretical framework in which to derive such a conclusion is "methodological naturalism", which is simply the assumption or *belief* that only the content of the natural (empirical) sciences is real. In other words, the conclusion is derived from a mere belief, and we have arrived back at the start of the discussion.

July 18, 2017

Blasphemy

13.   Atheists, if tomorrow it were proven beyond a shadow of a doubt that gods exist, would you want to remain an atheist? Why or why not?

Despite what one reads here, a large percentage of atheists will choose to remain atheists. This is because, being proselytizers for atheism (blasphemers) or supporters thereof, they sense that they are already lost and have nothing to lose by continuing to evince their contempt for, and implacable hatred of, the Almighty. (If equating "rationality" to hatred seems unjustified, the constantly fuming Richie Dawkins provides a clear example of antitheistic hatred masquerading as rationality.)

When the proof has been spelled out in a way that makes it absolutely inescapable for anyone with the high level of intelligence claimed by most atheists (who generally see themselves as rational skeptics and

"Brights"), it will be impossible for them to conceal their blasphemous intent even from themselves. Beholding themselves in the convoluted funhouse mirrors of their own disordered minds, transfixed by a final blinding burst of metacognitive presence restoring the true geometry of nature and exposing their implacable self-hatred, they will seal their own metaphysical fate.

But all is not yet lost. The good news is that self-styled atheists still capable of repentance can always mend their ways by their own volition, provided that they are willing to part ways with those who lack the sense to do so. And in any event, those who remain courageous and pure of heart need never despair, for the fires of hell warm the Kingdom of Heaven.

In the end, the books will balance. Atheists, including most of the Powers that Be, have a severe red-ink problem that only they can eliminate before the bill comes due, and this cannot be accomplished by disingenuous posturing or conforming to PC doctrine or writing checks to fashionable causes.

A word to the wise.

January 10, 2017

14.   Are there serious metaphysical consequences for unreasonably defaming the CTMU on Quora?

For those who have already severed their souls, amputating themselves from the identity of reality through blasphemy and moral atrophy, there are no further "metaphysical consequences". Barring an utterly heroic attempt at spiritual reconnection – the worse you are, the more heroic and costly the effort must be – the matter is completely settled, and divine "vindictiveness" has nothing to do with it.

I understand that the typical atheist, being a master thespian when it comes to empty bravado, will giggle like a tickled baby at the very thought. Oh, the sheer entertainment of it all!

But you know what they say: there are no atheists on deathbeds, at least who still have a choice about it.

So I'm afraid that it's laugh now, cry later … or perhaps that should be, wail and gnash your teeth later.

(Now, how will *that* be for entertainment? ;)

July 10, 2018

15. Are some atheists afraid of the CTMU?

Of course some atheists are afraid of the CTMU.

Which atheists, exactly? The more intelligent ones who have actually read and understood some appreciable part of it.

Their terror owes to the penalty that awaits them for the sacrilege and blasphemy with which they have systematically polluted the minds of entire generations, thereby parting them from the source of being and damning them to perdition.

September 23, 2018

CTMU attacks

16. Why are there atheists who criticize the CTMU without under-standing anything of it?

For essentially the same reason that someone might refuse to accept an apple as a piece of fruit because it fails to resemble an orange, banana, or kumquat.

As I've explained elsewhere on this site, true atheists actively disbelieve in God. (Despite the efforts of some to characterize themselves as "agnos-tic atheists", this phrase is nothing but an oxymoron demonstrating that they misunderstand not only the standard definitions of its constituent terms, but the relationship between faith and knowledge.) In many cases, this disbelief is so active that it becomes indistinguishable from virulent hatred, the nemesis of intellectual clarity and objectivity.

Let's have a closer look. Most atheists subscribe to (methodological or metaphysical) "naturalism", the dominant perspective in academia. For some of them, naturalism is more than just a perspective on reality; they see it as an *explanation* of reality. But as naturalism is fundamentally dualistic, destroying the connection between abstract and concrete reality, it doesn't work above a certain level of explanation; no coherent high-level explanation of reality can be fully interpreted in a naturalistic framework. Trying to do so anyway represents the height of confusion.

In contrast to naturalism, the CTMU is monic. When one tries to interpret a monic structure in a dualistic framework, one merely ends up ripping it in half, at which point one may fall through the gap that one has idiotically created between the resulting pieces, and then compounds the situation by complaining bitterly about it as though it's someone else's fault. This is the sad yet rather comical fate of many atheists who have tried and failed to understand the CTMU. They simply don't have a clue.

Obviously, I need not take responsibility for the intellectual shortcomings of atheists, which in some cases are both profound and numerous. They need to make at least a little effort to address their own conceptual deficiencies before running around making a lot of extremely unpleasant noise about things that they are incapable of comprehending.

February 12, 2018

17. Why do people still have atheistic leanings when the CTMU clearly proves that atheism is a priori false?

This recently posted question presently has 54 answers including this one, and another 38 which have been collapsed. I've gone through a few of these answers, and in addition to detecting quite a bit of nastiness, I've found that almost none of the authors displays the slightest knowledge of the theory they purport to be criticizing. Zero ... zilch ... nada.

Not much can be said on behalf of people who operate this way. One can't paint a smiley face on it. It's not as though these people are motivated by a love of truth and the advancement of knowledge; people who conform to that description at least acknowledge the content of that which they criticize.

The only explanation that seems reasonable at this point is that Quora is a dark carnival teeming with virulent atheistic-materialistic troll-clowns, and having driven off other potential targets with the insults and defamation for which they are famous, they are increasingly desperate for something, anything, to attack *en masse*. Hence, they've latched onto the CTMU like leeches, catapulting it to the status of premier troll-magnet at an already degenerate trollfest.

As I've pointed out before, I've never posted a question here (except to replace one that was erased after I'd already answered it), and I've never asked anyone else to post a question here. I've tried my best to provide sincere and informative answers for the questions I've encountered, that's all. But the troll attacks had begun before I even arrived (some even involved "Quora Top Writers"), they've only gotten worse as time has passed, and I'm starting to feel like the only surviving human in Zombie City. It's depressing.

Just in case any innocent, well-meaning naïf happens to bump into this feeding frenzy and mistakes it for a source of information, I'm advising you to avert your eyes. Most of it amounts to pseudointellectual hate-porn, and no decent person wants to dirty his or her eyes with it.

Thanks for your attention.

Addendum: There's something called an "Answer Wiki" at the top of this page. It is not accepting my edits, which is pretty much par for the course on this site, which is largely what makes this site a joke for purposes of getting anything properly established. My attempted addition read as follows:

> **Disputed by the author of the CTMU**. The undeniable fact is that those who express strong dislike of the theory typically fail to understand a single word of it – or at least so it appears from their failure to address its actual content – and the incomprehension often appears feigned rather than honest. Unfortunately, this is highly unlikely to change. Thanks for your attention.

As I say, this place seems to be nothing but an atheist-materialist troll-fest. What a shame.

July 9, 2018

Intolerance

18.   Is atheism a hoax?

Although atheism is non-factual, it is not a hoax. It exists as a (highly negative) theological doctrine, and many people actually believe in it despite the absence of anything approaching a proof that it is correct. That many atheists now occupy high places in the power structure, or exert pressure on those who do, has allowed them to do very real damage to the cultures and future prospects of Western nations and Western Civilization as a whole.

In contrast to many self-styled Christians who are passive to a fault, and who practice blanket tolerance of atheism on the absurd premise that the Bible somehow instructs them to do so, atheists tend to be highly intolerant, swarming outspoken theists and evincing the most vicious kinds of pack behavior, often attacking the good names, professional reputations, and livelihoods of their enemies. Yet despite their notoriety for this kind of mischief, atheists often characterize themselves as "moral" and "ethical", claiming that morality is independent of God. As this makes morality relative and thus neutralizes it – that's what it takes to explain why atheists embrace many different "moral codes" and definitions of morality – such assertions are preposterous.

This is why big-name atheists like Richard Dawkins and Daniel Dennett long ago settled on a policy of avoiding open dialogue with capable theists. Their stated rationale was transparently disingenuous: "Engaging with theists amounts to legitimizing them!" But of course, their real concern is that engaging with capable theists entails an unacceptably high risk of defeat and could eventually result in a resurgence of theism, an eventuality with which atheistic contempt and/or hatred for God is incompatible.

May 15, 2017

IQ level

19.   Why is it that atheism is prevalent amongst high IQ individuals?

The meaning of this question depends on that of "high IQ". Very high IQ individuals – those near the top of the scale – have not usually been atheistic, historically speaking. Atheism has usually been espoused by those whose levels of intelligence range from average to moderately above average, perhaps a bit higher in a few cases (e.g., Voltaire, who has often been claimed by atheists due to his attacks on religious authority, but would be better described as a deist who leaned toward the idea that the universe was intelligently designed).

July 4, 2018

20.   How do I stop being an atheist?

Spiritual understanding has two complementary aspects, faith and knowledge. The only real issue is which comes first, as you'll eventually need both. That is, to the extent that faith is true, it entails knowledge, and to the extent that someone who is rational must believe in that which one knows to be true, knowledge entails belief. (Recent atheistic attempts to couple and conflate atheism and agnosticism, e.g., the oxymoronic phrase "agnostic atheism" which seems to drive a wedge between knowledge and belief, are just a transparent ruse for which only fools can fall.)

Many atheists will tell you that there is "no logical or scientific reason" to believe in the existence of God, but they are mistaken. So the first thing you must do in your search for God is to disregard their opinions, which are in any case devoid of logical support. Remember, the vaunted correlation between atheism and IQ peters out above the "danger zone", where a danger-zone intellect is one that is sharp enough to be dangerous to ordinary people, but too dull to recognize and acknowledge its own limitations. (In contrast, when a very intelligent person has no support for his/her opinion, he/she wisely suspends judgment.)

Congratulations for realizing that atheism is something from which you need to escape. It's the first step toward spiritual understanding and redemption.

July 13, 2017

Irrationality

21.   Is atheism more logical than religion? If God doesn't exist, theism doesn't "lose", but if God in fact exists, atheist will suffer.

Spiritual understanding has two complementary aspects, faith and knowledge. The only real issue is which comes first, as you'll eventually need both. That is, to the extent that faith is true, it entails knowledge, and to the extent that someone who is rational must believe in that which one knows to be true, knowledge entails belief. (Recent atheistic attempts to couple and conflate atheism and agnosticism, e.g., the oxymoronic phrase "agnostic atheism" which seems to drive a wedge between knowledge and belief, are just a transparent ruse for which only fools can fall.)

Many atheists will tell you that there is "no logical or scientific reason" to believe in the existence of God, but they are mistaken. So the first thing you must do in your search for God is to disregard their opinions, which are in any case devoid of logical support. Remember, the vaunted correlation between atheism and IQ peters out above the "danger zone", where a danger-zone intellect is one that is sharp enough to be dangerous to ordinary people, but too dull to recognize and acknowledge its own limitations. (In contrast, when a *very* intelligent person has no support for his/her opinion, he/she wisely suspends judgment.)

Congratulations for realizing that atheism is something from which you need to escape. It's the first step toward spiritual understanding and redemption.

January 21, 2017

22.   How can someone be an atheist, if there is a chance there is a god? Because you can't prove there isn't, then when he dies he will find out he is doomed for eternity.

Being an atheist given the Biblical penalty for blasphemy is indeed very unwise. In fact, given that there is no proof of the nonexistence of God, it is irrational; professing atheism in spite of one's ignorance is like unnecessarily traversing a minefield in pitch blackness.

This irrationality is precisely how we know that atheism is not a mere abstract belief, instead amounting to active hatred of God. It is not for a mere lack of conviction that atheists are sentenced to hell; it is for actively, irrationally negating the existence of their own highest level of being. Obviously, those who are determined to negate their own being on the highest level thereof might as well forget about lower levels, which are automatically extinguished as a result. (Sad, isn't it.)

December 28, 2017

Irresolvable paradox

23. What important part of you was unlocked after becoming an atheist?

Becoming an atheist "unlocks" your capacity to embrace paradox. That is, it breaks you free of your psychological need for logical consistency, enabling you to embrace inconsistency as an integral component of your own psyche. This is not usually a good thing. In the context of God, it is in fact a *very* bad thing, as it deprives you of any sound basis for morality and disrupts your connection to reality.

As for the ridiculous idea that nothing is actually unlocked because atheism does not imply active belief in anything, the simple fact is that atheism *does* imply belief, specifically belief in the nonexistence of God. In other words, atheism means "actively disbelieving in God". "Not believing in God", on the other hand, is simply "non-theism".

Here's what amounts to a mathematical proof that atheists actively disbelieve in God. The word *atheism* can be etymologically deconstructed in two ways: *atheo + ism* and *a + theism*. The first literally means "belief in the nonexistence of God" (active disbelief in God), while the second means "nonbelief in the existence of God". But the second definition is not yet complete, because it fails to specify whether or not one believes in the *nonexistence* of God. If one does not believe in the nonexistence of God, then this amounts to plain old agnosticism, i.e., believing in *neither* the existence *nor* the nonexistence of God. Only if one actively believes in the nonexistence of God does the second definition cease to equate to agnosticism. In this case, one actively opposes God on the ontological level, and is that to which scripture refers as a "blasphemer".

Here's the bottom line: If you're a real atheist, then you actively disbelieve in God, and are therefore a blasphemer. Otherwise, you're just a plain old garden variety agnostic, in which case you shouldn't run around absurdly calling yourself an "atheist" or "agnostic atheist", as it would only cause others to question your intelligence (and eventually cause you even worse problems than that. ;)

I've already discussed this in several answers on this site. Feel free to look them up if this is still unclear to you.

October 21, 2017

24. Is Atheism as indefensible a position as believing in God is from a purely logical perspective? What do you think?

Atheism – the oxymoronic metaphysical statement that reality lacks a coherent metaphysical identity, which equates to "God" under certain definitions – is an irresolvable paradox. That is, it implicitly *affirms* its own truth while *denying* its own truth. A statement which is metaphysical by construction – i.e., which refers to nature or physical reality from above, occupying a higher level of reference – cannot be true where it explicitly denies its own metaphysical support.

In other words, atheism is too general in the kind of "God" it denies. Where a proper definition of God consists of logical necessities, a blanket denial of God renders itself paradoxical by negating these logical necessities. These necessities can be encapsulated in the necessary existence of a metaphysical identity (of reality), without which there can be no metaphysics, without which the metaphysical position of atheism – not to mention reality itself – cannot exist (because *existence* is a metaphysical and specifically an ontological function). On the other hand, theists who believe in "God" under this definition remain within the bounds of logic.

Many atheists are presently scrambling to sidestep logical objections to atheism by calling themselves "agnostic atheists". However, they might just as well drop the *atheist* from "agnostic atheist" and refer to themselves as *agnostics*. Given the way "agnostic atheism" is being promoted here on Quora (and elsewhere), it appears to be a disingenuous attempt to change the language so as to blur the distinction between atheists and agnostics.

What is the difference between atheism and agnosticism? Obviously, in order to distinguish between an *atheist* and a *non-atheist*, two questions must be answered: (1) "Do you believe in the **existence** of God?"; (2) "Do you believe in the **nonexistence** of God?" An agnostic answers NO to both questions; an atheist answers NO to 1 and YES to 2.

Failing to answer YES to question 2 while calling oneself an "atheist" amounts to declaring oneself *both* an atheist *and* an agnostic; the terms become effectively redundant. This fails to provide enough information to determine one's theological stance vis-a-vis the existence of God.

The only way around this is to claim that an atheist differs *epistemologically* from an agnostic, somehow "knowing" that *neither* the existence *nor* the nonexistence of God can be conclusively established. However, this too entails a burden of proof, and we don't see this burden being met.

So logically speaking, the bottom line is that where God is properly defined as the metaphysical identity of reality – and this can be done with a very high degree of logical precision – **theism beats atheism hands-down**.

May 30, 2018

Metaphysical naturalism

25.   Why haven't atheists started a belief system yet?

Because even the very best and most capable of them can be easily crushed by anyone who knows what he's doing. As any high-profile theist can attest, the closest the atheists have ever come to a coherent "theory of atheism" is the "theory" of insult, defamation, and dirty polemics to which so many of them resort after coming up short against someone more skilled at theological argumentation.

Their best "serious" attempt at a distinctively atheistic philosophical theory is called "metaphysical naturalism", which characteristically turns out to be an oxymoron. It holds that nothing exists but the "natural" (physical) objects, relations, and processes which form the content of the natural sciences. In other words, the metaphysical or "supernatural" is completely excluded from reality. Their decision to call what amounts to their ideological flagship "metaphysical naturalism" despite its exclusion of metaphysics stands as an everlasting testament to their collective theoretical incompetence.

Of course, it would be a mistake to suppose that all atheists are unintelligent. It's just that those who do most of the talking typically have psychological issues which occlude their powers of comprehension, sometimes including guilt and a fear of punishment, extreme intellectual narcissism, poor impulse control, emotional infantilism, and a defiant personality accompanied by a deep hatred of authority (especially religious authority).

July 8, 2017

26.   Does atheism entail metaphysical naturalism?

Superficially, atheism and metaphysical naturalism differ. The former merely excludes God from reality, while the latter excludes metaphysics, AKA "the supernatural", in its entirety (metaphysics is supernatural insofar as it refers to nature as a whole, and thus exists on a level above that of nature itself). But now let's see what logic has to say about it.

As far as logic is concerned, both metaphysical naturalism (the oxymoronic metaphysical statement that nature has no metaphysical aspect) and atheism (the ultimately equivalent and equally oxymoronic metaphysical statement that reality lacks a coherent metaphysical identity, which equates to "God" under pretty much any reasonable definition) are irresolvable paradoxes.[1] That is, they implicitly *affirm* their own truth while *denying* their own truth (because a statement which is metaphysical by construction – i.e., which refers to nature or physical reality from above – cannot be true where it explicitly denies its own metaphysical structure).

All irresolvable paradoxes are equivalent in the sense that they imply "True = False"; and where True = False, anything is true. In this sense, atheism entails metaphysical naturalism and vice versa.

Of course, any irresolvable paradox implies anything whatsoever. But what makes atheism and metaphysical naturalism so obvious as irresolvable paradoxes is the fact that they are oxymorons, i.e., paradoxical on their faces. Their inconsistency is not hidden, but as plain as day.

Only a fool could fall for either of them.

[**Note**: I see several answers here which claim that an atheist is simply a person who answers "no" to question (1): "Do you believe in the existence of god(s)?" This is disingenuous. There's another question that must be answered: (2) "Do you believe in the nonexistence of god(s)?" An atheist is someone who answers "no" to the first question and "yes" to the second.

Anyone who answers "no" to both questions is merely an *agnostic*. Claiming that only question 1 need be answered to distinguish an atheist

---

1   Atheism is paradoxical because it is too general in the kinds of "gods" it denies. In particular, where a proper definition of God consists of logical necessities, a blanket denial of God renders itself paradoxical by negating these logical necessities. These necessities can be encapsulated in the existence of a metaphysical identity of reality, without which there can be no metaphysics, without which the metaphysical position of atheism cannot exist.

from a non-atheist amounts to claiming that *atheism* and *agnosticism* mean the same thing. In fact, they have never meant the same thing and never will. It would be nice if atheists would stop trying to fool everyone about this.]

May 29, 2018

Social injustice

27.   If you are not accountable after death, you can do whatever you want to and get away with it. How do atheists defend this void of justice?

Most atheists conflate justice with legality. They maintain that evil is punished in the physical world "with a few exceptions" – after all, some criminals are sent to jail – and that deviations from justice are unavoidable but negligible.

However, in a world run by sociopaths, this is absurd. Sociopathic ruthlessness and dishonesty are systemic, being more often rewarded than punished (the more vile and audacious the better). We have war criminals in high office, mass murderers running the military-industrial-security complex, and galaxy-class thieves and extortionists running the banks and controlling the money supply. Their corruption and injustice are contagious; using government as a means of control, they write laws under which anyone who refuses to go along is economically disenfranchised, incarcerated, or killed. Injustice is thus self-reinforcing, eventually becoming the norm.

It follows that an atheist who considers himself "rational" has no choice but to deny that justice exists in any necessary sense, thus voiding any responsibility to explain its absence. And as the concept of justice flies out the window, so does any enforceable basis for morality, thus reducing phrases like "moral atheist" and "atheistic morality" to meaninglessness.

July 17, 2017

BELIEFS

Non-believing

28. What do you call someone when they don't believe in God, Satan, Jesus and religion?

This question is all over the place. If one does not believe in the existence of Satan, then one can be called (e.g.) "a non-follower of any religion incorporating the concept of Satan". If one does not believe in the sayings of Jesus, then one can be called (e.g.) a "non-Christian" and a "non-Muslim". If one does not believe in the existence of Jesus, then one can be called (e.g.) a "non-follower of any Abrahamic religion". If one does not believe in the existence of God *qua* Logos (essentially, logic), then one can be called (e.g.) "illogical" or "irrational"; if one does not believe in God under any definition, then one can be called (e.g.) "atheistic" or "agnostic". If one does not believe in any religion at all, then one can be called (e.g.) "irreligious". If one does not believe in the very existence of religion, then one can be called (e.g.) "delusional". If one does not believe in any of these things, then one can be described as all of the above (and more, very little of it complimentary. ;)

June 11, 2017

BIOLOGY

Evolutionary biologists

29.   Why do some evolutionary biologists belittle supporters of Intelligent Design and Creationism?

For several reasons. First, many of them – despite being relatively knowledgeable about some of the mechanisms involved in evolutionary biology – do not understand that the issue of ultimate origins is not strictly scientific, but metaphysical by definition. Some of them even dispute the very existence of metaphysics, subscribing to an oxymoronic philosophy called "metaphysical naturalism" which, despite its name, effectively denies that nature has a metaphysical aspect. In order to get away with it, they simply replace the word *metaphysical* with *supernatural*, and under what they imagine to be the deep cover of this transparent semantic switcheroo, absurdly issue what amounts to a metaphysical injunction against "the supernatural".

Secondly, many evolutionary biologists are hostile toward religion, and even though ID is not defined in religious terms – it is innocuously defined as "the theory that life, or the universe, cannot have arisen by chance and somehow involves the application of intelligence" – everything looks like a nail to people with nothing but a hammer. I learned this the hard way many years ago, when I was hounded all over the Internet by trolls accusing me of being an "Intelligent Design Creationist" when I actually had a preexisting theory that bears no resemblance to the stock ID theory promoted by the ID Movement. Once a surfeit of these unpleasant creatures fixate on you, crouch like skunks, and let fly in your direction with page after page of insult, venom, and illogical nonsense, they don't stop. The spray continues to exit their reeking rear ends until their hostility is accidentally refocused by, e.g., a major natural disaster occurring in their immediate vicinity.

Thirdly, some people get their jollies by putting on exhibitions of spite, and certain less talented academic scientists have learned how to attract unmerited attention and approval by engaging in pack behavior, mocking and belittling those attacked by their more eminent colleagues in the hope that a bit of prestige will trickle down on them. No, it's not nice, and it's not pretty to watch. But anyone who thinks that those who specialize in "debunking ID" are driven or inhibited by insight, compassion, or cold scientific rationality needs to pry the tube of model airplane glue from one's nose and suck down a hot cup of coffee.

This comedy will continue until the dialogue is shifted into its proper context, which is presently understood by neither side of the debate. But to judge from the incredible tenacity of those who latched onto "ID Creationism" twenty years ago like rabid badgers and have never since managed to let go of it or even gain an inch of perspective on it, it's probably not a good idea to hold one's breath.

May 10, 2018

COMMUNICATION

Barriers of communication

30.   What are some examples of the barriers of communication?

The first step is to classify the requirements of communication and the possible causes of failure.

Communication is the transfer of information (a message) from a sender to one or more receivers; hence, any problem with the form of the message (encryption, improper syntax, semantic degeneracy, etc.), or the mental or computational state, structure, or dynamics of sender or receiver, impairs it. One also needs a medium and channel for the transfer; if the medium is deficient or too high in entropy, or the channel is blocked or subject to excessive noise or interference, communication is impaired. The content of any message must be placed in a properly layered context, up to and including the language in which it expressed, which may be limited in its expressive capacity or designed and utilized for deception and control rather than honest communication. Obviously, if the message contains lies (content is corrupt), or if it must be understood in an ambiguous context or in the context of a false narrative or body of false doctrine (context is corrupt), a communication problem exists.

Now here's the really bad part. (1) Largely because governments, corporations, and social engineers (including academia and the mass media), who are self-serving and ethically confused or uninhibited, work under the (often accurate) assumption that people and society can be controlled by twisting and manipulating information and communication, we are presently dealing with all of these problems in spades. (2) These problems render democracy, scientific progress, and a proper understanding of reality all but impossible, guaranteeing the continued political, socio-economic, and psychological degeneration of mankind.

[Of course, there is a more "touchy-feely" interpretation of this question which might be better expressed as "What are the psycho-social barriers between human beings which can impair their ability to express or understand each other's thoughts, feelings, and intentions?" The answer would obviously include every source of emotional conflict and personal confusion known to man, complicated by every personality disorder and combination of psychological traits and circumstances under the sun.]

May 24, 2017

COMPUTER SCIENCE

Self-simulation

31.   What does the CTMU contribute to the field of computer science, especially artificial intelligence?

Regarding computer science, CTMU originally stood for "Computation Theoretic Model of the Universe" before it was extended to encompass the entirety of cognition. It is by far the most advanced theory of reality as a self-simulation; other so-called "simulation theories" are beneath comparison.

Regarding AI, the CTMU is not about "artificial" intelligence. It is about *real* intelligence, including *synthetic* intelligence. Anything less is just the race to make money by selling rope to the would-be hangmen of mankind in the form of mechanical golems that can be used to subvert, suppress, and manipulate human cognition, communication, and action.

September 5, 2018

CONSCIOUSNESS

Consciousness and life

32.   What do you think came first, consciousness or life?

Neither; they come as one. Attempting to define either without using the other as a definitional parameter is meaningless; they have an irreducible semantic overlap.

Of course, the linguistic operation of definition leaves much room for creativity. If one likes, one can simply define these two terms, *consciousness* and *life*, in any of four ways: (1) they are mutually independent; (2) life depends on consciousness, but not vice versa; (3) consciousness depends on life, but not vice versa; (4) they come bound together in mutual dependency. But then one faces the problem of mapping one's definition to reality, and that's where one can run into trouble.

Obviously, condition 1 equates to **Cartesian mind-body dualism**, with consciousness standing for *mind* and life standing for *body*. That's a no-go, as it precludes any meaningful relationship between the two. There's simply no way to hold them together in a single unified reality such as the one we inhabit.

Condition 2 is almost right, but there's a problem: consciousness – understood simplistically as "self-awareness" – immediately requires that an entity have dual aspects: (a) that aspect which is subjectively aware, and (b) that aspect which is the object of subjective awareness. This self-duality immediately implies a view of reality (the CTMU) in which life and consciousness are "metasimultaneous" in the sense of condition 4.

Condition 3, the "emergence" of consciousness from certain physical phenomena to which "life" has been attributed by definition, is the dominant view in academia and elsewhere. Unfortunately, it is absurd insofar as it merely amounts to the supervenience of mind on physical substance and process, and thus equates to physicalism – or if one prefers the conventional oxymoron, "metaphysical naturalism" – which in effect denies the distinction between mind and matter, or consciousness and life, while implicitly claiming that the latter (physicality) has priority.

Finally, we have condition 4, which is true by implication (condition

2) and elimination of conditions 1 and 3. As previously mentioned, this requires a new paradigm called the CTMU (*Cognitive Theoretic Model of the Universe*) in which *life* and *consciousness* have a higher form of simultaneity, *metasimultaneity*, which is technically defined within the theory.

[**Note regarding the standard physicalistic view of emergence** (condition 3): Obviously, substance does not exist apart from its properties. Properties *characterize* substance, which *instantiates* properties. Given any substance, its properties are what lend it form and make it discernible from the general environment; therefore, it cannot stand alone as the source from which its properties emerge. Its properties cannot "supervene" on it, or "emerge" from it, unless the dependency can be reversed so that the substance is regarded as supervening on/emerging from its properties.

This amounts to saying that any process of emergence requires a "syntax" (formal structure, generic metaproperty) implicitly containing all of the possible properties of any substance that can instantiate them. In other words, for a property like *consciousness* to emerge from living matter (the substance which instantiates it), that property must "already" be implicit in syntax (as must the properties *living* and *materiality*), in which case it is just as true that living matter is a function of consciousness.

Therefore, condition 3 – as understood in the context of physicalism – is ultimately absurd. Stock physicalism ("mind supervenes on matter, but not vice versa") is ontologically inconsistent, and *emergence* must be defined as it is in the CTMU (condition 4).]

May 22, 2018

Hard problem of consciousness

33. How does Chris Langan's CTMU (Cognitive-Theoretic Model of the Universe) address the "hard problem of consciousness"?

By formulating the structure of reality in a monic, self-dual way.

Remember, the "Hard Problem" is really just a formulation of Cartesian mind-matter dualism. What's "hard" (in fact, impossible) about it is the insistence that it can be properly resolved only while leaving its central assumption intact, i.e., the irrational insistence that it be answered entirely within the constraints of dualism, or somewhat equivalently, physicalism.

The CTMU "short-circuits" the problem by expressing the structure of reality in a self-dual (dual-aspect monic) ontological framework. This causes it to vanish by denying it the conventional dualistic framework in which it is improperly formulated.

February 4, 2018

CONSPIRACY THEORIES

Coudenhove-Kalergi Plan

34.   Is the Kalergi plan a conspiracy theory?

Of course it is, on two counts.

First, the Coudenhove-Kalergi Plan is a *conspiracy* involving the European ruling class and the international bankers on whom its members have always relied for money to fund their wars, colonial adventures, and so on.

Secondly, the Coudenhove-Kalergi Plan is a conspiracy *theory* because it has rightly been called a "conspiracy" by others. In other words, it is the object of a *theory* externally formed *about* a conspiracy.

A little background. War loans are a very profitable business for international bankers, who get to fund, and collect, from both sides of every conflict. The winner pays willingly because it extorts reparations from the loser, and the loser pays because those reparations have been doubled in order to ensure it (and because losers can also be dunned directly by their "loan officers").

And of course, wars and colonial adventures can also be very good for heads of state, high-ranking military officers, and those who profit from the manufacture of weaponry and munitions (eventually dubbed "the Military-Industrial Complex" by US President and former General Dwight D. Eisenhower). And let's not forget multinational corporations supplying the military and engaging in international trade.

It follows that these groups have a *motive* for conspiracy, namely, prospective gains of money and power. It also follows that they have *means* and *opportunity*, which follows immediately from *already having* most of the wealth and power. It even follows that they must lie about their actual motives, lest the populace rise up against them and take their money and power away from them. Their collusion and secrecy, often rationalized in terms of "national security", establishes that they are implicated in a *conspiracy* for which they possess means, motive, and opportunity.

As explained by Coudenhove-Kalergi himself in *Praktischer Idealismus* (1925), and even considerably earlier in the associated movement, the idea was to:

(1) Blame the indigenous people of Europe for European war and colonization ("Indigenous Europeans are congenitally greedy, quarrelsome, and violent!") despite the fact that unlike European royalty and the bankers who funded their various wars, the vast majority of Europeans had never seen a bit of the money or territory gained in such adventures at the cost of their lives, limbs, and happiness in their otherwise peaceful and productive societies, using this false pretext to justify the elimination of European cultural and ethnic (genetic) identity by means of politics and mass immigration and its unavoidable consequences including transformative effects on European population genetics;

(2) Intermix and communize the resulting deracinated population, depriving them of their ethnic and cultural identities in order to thoroughly domesticate them and prepare them for global governance under the enlightened leadership of the bankers and despots who had actually been guilty of starting, funding, and profiting from all of the wars and colonial misadventures for which the innocent masses of Europe had been falsely blamed;

(3) Justify permanent control of the resulting divided-and-conquered population, a so-called "Eurasian-Negroid Race of the Future", by a "Master Race" consisting of, you guessed it, a combination of European royalty and international bankers and their friends and progeny (which, owing to its supposed moral and intellectual superiority, would not be subject to genetic dilution).

This is all in print, in the abovementioned book and elsewhere. There's simply no denying it, at least if one has any respect for the truth. The movement was handsomely funded by famous international bankers including Warburg and Rothschild and eagerly embraced by European royalty ... i.e., by the other (non-banking) constituents of the "Master Race", which today controls the EU economy and EU immigration policy.

Notice that this policy is exactly, precisely what Coudenhove-Kalergi prescribed in *Praktischer Idealismus*, and that the despotic, undemocratic bureaucrats of the EU take all of their orders strictly from above, i.e., from members of the EU "Master Race". So there is no question that what we see today is a perfect reflection of what the movement prescribed.

R.N. Coudenhove-Kalergi, founder of the Pan-European movement and often called the "Father of the European Union", was the winner of the EU's first Charlemagne Prize. He even chose the EU anthem. There is no question whatsoever that those who run the EU embraced his program completely and continue to do so.

Note that the ultimate success of this program would result in a 2-tier society consisting of an inbred, filthy-rich overclass and an impoverished, genetically homogenized underclass inhabiting what amounts to a "world-hive". In such a hivelike arrangement, war and colonization would no longer be necessary for the royalty-banker "Master Race" to remain in control. The hive would contain workers, drones, and soldiers to police the workers and drones 24/7 and squeeze them for every last drop of blood on behalf of their masters, no wars necessary except for purposes of population control.

[If you want to argue about this, please don't expect me to engage with you on it. As far as I'm concerned – and many others share my opinion – these are well-documented facts and thus bear no debate.]

September 21, 2018

Powers that be

35. What is the most ludicrous scientific or political conspiracy theory?

The idea that legions of wingnuts, fruitcakes, and outhouse rats are "out to get" the powers-that-be by accusing them of collusion and conspiracy when in reality, the powers-that-be are enlightened and uniformly benign entities who always tell the truth, obey the law, and want what's best for everyone else even if they must nobly sacrifice themselves on our behalf.

A bit of reflection should quickly reveal who the real "wingnuts, fruitcakes, and outhouse rats" are here. The fact is that whenever a potential conspiracy has positive mathematical expectation, those in a position to execute it and reap its rewards will almost always attempt to do so. (It's called "human nature".) Obviously, those most often in this position are the powers-that-be.

Beware the indoctrination victim who denies this aspect of reality. Such people are dangerous in the extreme.

May 11, 2018

Secret organizations

36.   Could secret organizations exist?

Yes. Otherwise, why would there be a legal concept called "criminal conspiracy", defined as an agreement between two or more parties to commit an unlawful act? As the act is unlawful, the conspirators generally keep their agreement secret to avoid being arrested. So by definition, almost any criminal conspiracy qualifies as a "secret organization". (Conversely, many secret organizations amount to criminal conspiracies.)

Nevertheless, many people would answer this question negatively for fear of harassment. In this day and age, daring to call out the members of a conspiracy is likely to get one mocked and ostracized as a "conspiracy theorist". But this is absurd, for well-designed conspiracies occasion more gain than risk for those in a position to keep their secrets. Such people often find conspiracy economically and/or politically rational, a fact which virtually guarantees its widespread existence.

One example of a gainful but very secret organization was the Italian Mafia, whose existence was admitted only relatively recently. There have been countless others, up to and including hidden layers of government.

March 21, 2018

CONSTRUCTION

Cold joint

37.   What are the effects of a concrete cold joint?

The effects may be classified as structural, functional, and cosmetic. Structurally, a cold joint or cold seam is weaker than the surrounding concrete and thus a potential plane of fracture. Functionally, it can result in difficulty working the concrete, causing waviness of the surface, and as a result, difficulty in closing seams between floors and walls and (in extreme cases) potential loss of footing. Cosmetically, a cold joint can result in an unsightly, highly visible linear discoloration which will not stain properly, and the extra difficulty of working the concrete due to reduced plasticity of the older section can lead to visible surface imperfections (rips, tears, bubbles, pits, grooves, scuffs, and so on along the joint) which may require expensive sanding and polishing to repair.

In short, cold joints are bad news, and are only weakly mitigated by dense steel reinforcement (plenty of rebar in the concrete). A concrete supplier whose delivery intervals are known to be so long that they could produce cold joints should not be hired. Adding retardant to the concrete can help, but only up to a point.

May 13, 2017

CTMU

Academic reception

38. Could Chris Langan's CTMU just be one big ploy to demonstrate the gullibility of academics?

Hmmm ... I wonder. After all, we have the Sokal debacle to consider. But if so, then to judge from the number of academics who have expressed interest over the years, one would think that academia had "passed the test". On the other hand, one might also think that some courageous academic big shot who actually knows what he's doing in the field would have stepped forward to either hit the CTMU with a knockout punch, or take a hard shot on the chin and get put on his smug, self-satisfied ass by it. (My money's on the CTMU. ;)

December 28, 2017

Algebraic algorithms

39. What would Christopher Langan's Cognitive-Theoretic Model of the Universe look like if it was reduced to an algebraic algorithm?

The phrase "algebraic algorithm" is perhaps inappropriate in this context, if only because it is too limiting. (Algorithms are problem-solving procedures which always have algebraic aspects, but are generally of limited applicability.) On the other hand, as a mathematical structure which "solves the problem of describing and explaining reality", the CTMU looks like any number of abstract structures which have been explicated in numerous essays, web pages, and academic papers on the CTMU (complex problems often require complex solutions).

February 14, 2018

Comprehending CTMU

40.   Why don't people understand the CTMU?

Some people have difficulty understanding the CTMU because they spend no significant amount of time trying to absorb the maximally simplified language in terms of which the theory has been described. While it contains neologisms (as does almost any new and original theory), standard terminology is nowhere redefined in it, so those confused by it cannot point to linguistic usage as a reason to dismiss it.

As the CTMU has been designed as a comprehensive theoretical framework for reality at large, it cannot be reduced or condensed in any way that would diminish its intended scope. By the same token, introducing such a theory requires that one explain why the overall worldview it replaces is deficient, which unfortunately can easily be mistaken for the claim that "all that has gone before it is wrong" (*deficient* need not mean "wrong"; it can also mean "incomplete").

In fact, the CTMU has been designed so that all valid scientific theories can be modeled within it.

May 20, 2018

CTMU vs atheistic globalists

41.   When will the CTMU finally take off?

In all likelihood, the CTMU will take off when the avenues of intellectual commerce are no longer monopolized and dominated by people who perceive the CTMU as antithetical to their interests. Unfortunately, this dominance has been globally bureaucratized through Academia, Inc., which is itself thoroughly dominated by atheistic progressive globalists. At this point in history, the global bureaucracy has a great deal of momentum; the ownership and enslavement of the planet has been its primary incentive for quite some time, and the resulting damage to society is cumulative and ongoing. Obviously, it is not up to me alone to break this momentum.

I suggest that people who want the CTMU to "take off" should consider doing a little something to help this happen, as opposed to sitting around, carping about it, and overloading fora like this one with *ad hominem* attacks on its author (me). I do more for humanity every day by upholding and developing the structure of reality than the entire set of CTMU critics could do for humanity in a lifetime of bitter, confused bellyaching about it.

January 12, 2018

Defining usefulness

42.   What's the most useful and tangible consequence of the CTMU (Cognitive-Theoretic Model of the Universe)? What is an example of a way the CTMU has changed or altered one's life in a real way?

"Useful" to whom, and for what?

Some people consider a basic understanding of reality psychologically and socially useful and even indispensable for the health of individuals and societies. (They're right.) Once people are equipped with such knowledge, they can choose to apply it in more or less obvious ways, using it to guide and parameterize ethical judgments and personal, political, educational, and administrative decisions. (Of course, problems can arise for those who are completely uncreative, and need certified acadummies to explain to them, for up to several hundred thousand dollars over the course of a university education, how to think. Such people naturally have our sympathies.)

Others want new gadgets or substances that they can use for various more specific purposes. The "cooler" the substance or device and its applications, the better. (It's a shame when people find themselves unable to evaluate utility in any other way than by using teenage vernacular like "cool", but that's the world we inhabit.) Yet others want to run the companies that manufacture such substances and devices in order to make "buttloads" of money and be *really* cool. (Nothing like a bit of super-cool "disruptive tech" to become filthy rich and preside over your own personal empire even if you're just a greedy, self-serving sociopath who had to steal it!) Others, already rich and powerful, may want new tech just for the purpose of sitting on it so as not to disrupt their own income streams (or major rivers), which they have monopolized and which may involve inferior tech with a great deal of economic inertia. (Talk about greedy, self-serving sociopaths!)

But here's the real problem with gadgets and disruptive tech: if there is anything about any given device or substance or technology that can be weaponized or abused for profit or pleasure, it will be. This is a virtual certainty in today's shallow, hedonistic, and highly competitive world, and what it comes down to is this: if there's any way at all for one's "cool" inventions to circle around and bite one in the derriere, or bite society in the derriere, one can start the countdown and time it on one's watch!

Fortunately, a proper understanding of reality comes without this major drawback. Some people would call that a very good thing. (They're right.)

[Note: I just received an automatic notification advising me to "add a credential" in order to help my readers. Rushing to comply, I entered "Sole Author of the CTMU", which is absolutely true about me and potentially very helpful for those seeking correct information on the CTMU, which after all is clearly mentioned in the question. But this "credential" is not being displayed. The reason given by Quora: "This credential is hidden and needs editing to be helpful to readers. Please edit and improve it to have it appear next to your answers." I have no idea what this seemingly idiotic instruction is supposed to mean. Therefore, no credential. Thank you for your attention.]

March 20, 2018

Evaluating CTMU

43. Why are many physicists incompetent when it comes to evaluating Christopher Langan's Cognitive-Theoretic Model of the Universe?

There are a number of CTMU papers online, every one of which clearly states one or more problems and then solves or explores them.

Perhaps the most general encapsulation would be: "The CTMU solves the scientific, mathematical, and philosophical problems attending Cartesian dualism by instead placing these disciplines within a form of dual-aspect monism, thus supplanting dualism with self-duality."

Most physicists are trained to make sense of neither this problem nor its solution, both of which are very important to physics as a whole. Depending on their specialties, this does not necessarily make them "incompetent" as physicists. However, it obviously makes them incompetent to criticize the CTMU, especially in a casual or peremptory way.

Fortunately, a great many physicists have the general intellectual competence to refrain from opposing what they are unequipped to comprehend. This works greatly in their favor, as they avoid denying crucial implications of physical science.

February 11, 2018

Logical integrity

44. To all those with IQ scores above 150, what is your take on the CTMU?

I'm fairly well-known for having an IQ well above 150, and I also have the advantage of being the author of the CTMU. Not only is the CTMU the only theory of reality with complete logical integrity, but any other theory of reality which cannot be wholly interpreted in the CTMU – i.e., mapped into it on all orders with complete preservation of structure – is erroneous.

No one has ever succeeded in both exhibiting any understanding of what the CTMU actually says, and finding an error in it. This is because the CTMU has been structured in such a way that no errors are logically possible. (Bear in mind that the CTMU does not rely on empirical methodology, from which nothing can be definitively established beyond the level of direct perception, but instead utilizes a new kind of metalogical inference to justify itself.)

January 6, 2018

Meaning of life

45.   Does your CTMU include a theory for the meaning of life? If it does, what does it suggest? Is it for us to create ourselves, or are you seeking the fundamental reason for existence?

The CTMU is a theory of the meaning of life. "Meaning" is how things relate to each other; a bit more abstractly, it is the existence and evolution of relational structure and structure-preserving morphisms. Where relational structure is referred to as "identity", it is thus about the expression and evolution of identity on all levels of reality at large. For a human individual, the general idea is to exist and evolve consistently on all levels of identity, through the family, group, social, species, planetary, and cosmic levels all the way up to the spiritual level.

Note that those who deny the spiritual (top) level of identity might as well not even think about real meaning, as it is simply not in their prospectus (except insofar as it might be imposed on them from without, e.g., as when their employers deem them tools and wage-slaves, politicians deem them voters and useful idiots, the government deems them cannon-fodder and sources of tax revenue, and their bankers deem them chattel or "useless eaters"). Sadly, the dominant ideology among such people – be it called naturalism, physicalism, secularism, atheism, or whatever they like – fails to incorporate a coherent top-level identity, which means that when it comes down to lower dependent levels of identity, they might as well hang it up.

It thus goes without saying that if you want your life to have meaning, you'd better get straight with the metaphysical structure of reality and your own ultimate spiritual identity. The CTMU exists to help you do that.

(Incidentally, I'm the author of the CTMU. Accept no substitutes.)

February 10, 2018

Metaformal system

46.   Why is Langan's CTMU not a real theory?

This question is not valid; it is not meant to inform, but to impugn. There is no one anywhere who can show that the CTMU is "not a theory", and anyone who makes this claim is a fraud.

The CTMU is a *new and very advanced* kind of theory, but the differences between the CTMU and ordinary theories make it stronger rather than weaker. Instead of being a mere body of empirical-inductive speculation haphazardly glued onto one or more formal systems which serve as its theoretical backbone, the CTMU is a metaformal system in which language and universe are combined using the property of intelligibility. It is the only theory of its kind, and deserves applause rather than unpleasant insinuations.

(One obviously biased CTMU question posted for purposes of harassment; six pejorative and misinformative answers posted by people who, to judge by what they have written, know absolutely nothing about the theory itself. What a site!)

September 28, 2018

Metalogical system

47.   In which sense is Christopher Langan's Cognitive-Theoretic Model of the Universe mathematical, meta-mathematical, logical and metalogical?

The CTMU is logical and mathematical because it explicitly contains logical and mathematical structures, concepts, and reasoning. The CTMU is metalogical and metamathematical because it is reflexively self-modeling or distributively closed under valid interpretation, mapping the correspondence between itself and its universe of discourse and describing the relationship between logico-mathematical syntax and the real phenomena to which it applies.

March 7, 2018

Metaphysical formulation of logic

48.   Is CTMU an introduction to metaphysics?

No, the CTMU is not formulated on a mere "introductory" level. It is metaphysics at its most advanced, with a powerful and unique design that only trolls and metaphysical ignoramuses are foolish enough to contradict. It has been repeatedly published in reputable academic journals, and has withstood every informed critique ever leveled against it. Its structure is that of a metaphysical formulation of truth and logic themselves; hence, it is not open to doubt and will never be superseded by a "better" theory.

March 28, 2018

Metaphysical metalanguage

49.   What is the relationship between science, religion, and logic?

It is called the **CTMU** (*Cognitive-Theoretic Model of the Universe*), it has been around since the 1980's, it was authored by me (Christopher Langan), it is absolutely superior in every way to every other theory of its kind, and it is written in stone (very *hard* stone).

The CTMU comprises a metaphysical formulation of *logic* which has the form of a special scientific and theological metalanguage that takes both scientific theories and bodies of religious belief as object languages, and in which *science* and *religion* require interpretation for mutual and self-consistency. Modeling each of these classes of object language in the CTMU leads to their convergence, eliminating much of the conceptual distance between them.

In other words, the relationship in question takes the form of a logical language in which scientific and religious truth can be expressed and related, and the structure of this language is already a well-solved problem.

May 24, 2018

50.   Does the CTMU show that some religious ideas can be critically examined with metaphysical logic?

Yes, it does. That's because it is a metaphysical metalanguage with unique logical support for the expression of religious and spiritual concepts such as God, the human soul, the nature of good and evil, alternate realms of spiritual existence, and the relationship between life and death.

Lesser languages – e.g., physicalism, metaphysical naturalism, and comparable pseudo-philosophical conceptual frameworks – lack such support. This is why people who insist that reality is all and only "physical" often reject spiritual and religious concepts across the board.

Where the limits of one's language are also the limits of one's powers of comprehension, spiritual and religious concepts are utterly inconceivable to those from whose cognitive languages metaphysics has been excluded.

July 14, 2018

Next calculus

51.   What is the "next calculus," meaning what is, if there is one, its 21st century analog?

The CTMU (Cognitive-Theoretic Model of the Universe). Based on a powerful, highly sophisticated, and unique mathematical structure, it's a way to link mathematical formalisms with their contents (the things which model them in various ways). It has been out there for around thirty (30) years. Its author was introduced at the turn of the millennium as "the smartest man in America / the world" on every major US television network, along with many other major media outlets abroad. It has never been successfully challenged.

Sadly for those who depend on Academia for mathematical and empirical-scientific insight, academic interest in the CTMU remains minimal to nonexistent. It's not that Academia has anything better or more important or useful on which to concentrate; it's just that Academia has been corporatized, has established a virtual monopoly on scientific communication and intellectual commerce, and no longer has any incentive whatsoever to entertain contributions from outside sources.

June 3, 2017

Nonspeculative character

52.   Is the CTMU theory of Chris Langan provable or a speculation?

There's nothing speculative about the CTMU. (For the answers to questions like this one, feel free to go through the many CTMU-related answers I've already posted here.)

May 10, 2018

Paradigm shift

53.   It has been stated that "if you can't explain it simply, you don't understand it well enough." Can Christopher Langan explain his Cognitive-Theoretic Model of the Universe (CTMU) simply?

Obviously, "simple" is a relative term. Something which may be unfathomably complex to a monkey – integral calculus, for example – might be very easy for a more intelligent creature, e.g. a moderately intelligent human being, to grasp. This general situation applies throughout the entire range of variation of intelligence and complexity. In short, the meaning of "simple" depends on intelligence and intelligence differentials.

Just as obviously to anyone who is both intelligent and well-motivated enough to have familiarized himself / herself with my published work before criticizing it, I have given what I consider very simple, very straightforward explanations of the CTMU. Unfortunately, certain people persist in claiming that they are too complex to be understood ... and just to make sure that no one misses their displeasure, these people run around posting their disappointment to various social media, sometimes seeming to cross the boundary which separates honest, constructive criticism from trolling.

My honest impression is that either my simplifications have remained too complex for certain people to understand given their best efforts to do so, OR certain people didn't really make their best effort to make sense of them. For example, perhaps certain people rejected my explanations because accepting them would have forced them to let go of something dear to them, e.g., atheism. (I need scarcely mention that it would be inappropriate for me to apologize to such people, as in this case, the fault lies entirely with them.)

This being understood, the CTMU represents a major paradigm shift. The thing about paradigms is that they have a great deal of inertia, comprising underlying models in which people implicitly interpret what they read and hear. Thus, paradigm shifts are obstructed by the conceptual inertia of existing paradigms. In academia, the prevailing paradigm is "naturalism", which in various contexts is synonymous with physicalism, materialism, and even secularism. I think the problem here may be that some people are so cognitively invested in this paradigm that they unwittingly attempt to interpret proposed alternatives in the very cognitive framework which those alternatives are designed to replace, thus sabotaging their own comprehension.

I hope this helps, if only a little. Rest assured that I intend to keep trying – even when a person who is drowning goes into an irrational panic and ignores the life preserver he/she is thrown, the rescuer still has the option of jumping into the water, physically subduing him, and making him wear it. (It's either that, or the victim might actually drown. ;)

January 7, 2018

54. Why do people have such a hard time understanding the Cognitive-Theoretic Model of the Universe by Chris Langan?

Different people no doubt have different reasons for their confusion regarding the CTMU. Some lack the background to understand it, and are unwilling to put forth the time and effort needed to remedy this situation; others feel threatened by the prospect that the CTMU will displace some cherished belief such as atheism or materialism.

But perhaps the most general reason is that the CTMU represents a new paradigm for the human conception of reality, and new paradigms cannot be fully understood in terms of the old paradigms which they replace. It follows that paradigm shifts are resisted by people who, unwittingly or by preference, cling to old paradigms.

January 12, 2018

55. Will the CTMU of Chris Langan become the most important theory of humankind?

There are many important theories which deservedly occupy places in the sun. But as time inevitably passes and minds evolve, the weather changes. At this point, the once-productive "naturalistic" worldview on which most of our dominant theories are based has gone no-frills, stone-cold, pockets-turned-inside-out, can't-squeeze-blood-from-a-turnip bankrupt.

In short, the formerly successful theories that scientists and philosophers are still trying to use in order to answer their most profound questions have proven to be abject failures for that purpose. (They're still quite useful for some problems, mind you, but not for the biggest ones.) We're not just talking "the jury isn't in yet"; we're talking "not even within broadcast range of anything approaching a real answer." It has been that way for quite a while now, and only the infants among us are still denying it.

When such a situation arises – as it has arisen at several past junctures in human intellectual history – the only possible remedy is a paradigm shift. The CTMU is indeed a paradigm shift, and it does indeed resolve many of the issues plaguing the dominant worldview. We may thus infer that the CTMU is unsurpassed in its importance to the continued progress and future history of science and philosophy.

Of course, the problem with any paradigm shift is that almost everyone invested in the current paradigm idiotically tries to cram the new one into it, and when it proves a bad fit, they squawk like singed boobies. Attempting to shoehorn a new paradigm into the old one it is designed to replace is generally an exercise in futility, potentially leading to a Galileo-versus-the-Church situation.

Just be patient. Even infants must one day become adults.

June 23, 2018

Predictions

56.   Does Chris Langan's CTMU give rise to any kind of physical predictions that could be experimentally tested? Is any part of it potentially falsifiable?

Yes, the CTMU is as empirically falsifiable as any scientific theory. For example, it predicts the apparent accelerating expansion of the universe, and is therefore confirmed by the corresponding "observation statement" (a statement which affirms the empirical content of an observation).

However, owing to model-theoretic ambiguity, it is not always possible to empirically distinguish between two explanatory theories with respect to a given observation statement or prediction. In such cases, it is necessary to replace empirical confirmation with a more unequivocal standard, that of logical verification. This is where the CTMU shines, putting all competition out of the running (except insofar as "the competition" is really just a recapitulation of the CTMU after all).

This may be hard to understand without a little background. First, with respect to anything but directly observed data and their logical implications, the phrase "empirical falsifiability" is an oxymoron. No theory with nontrivial content is either empirically verifiable or falsifiable unless it is either limited to a universe that is already completely known (in which case it is scientifically redundant and superfluous), or formulated in such a way that it is possible, at least in principle, to observe a direct counterexample or make an observation from which a contradiction of the theory can be logically inferred.

For example, say that you have a theory which asserts that all crows are black. (Note the involvement here of what is called *universal quantification* in predicate logic.) It is possible to empirically falsify this theory by observing a single non-black crow, e.g., an albino crow, or perhaps a crow with feathers that have been bleached and dyed. But unless one's theory deals with some aspect of reality that is both observable and absolute or universal, it is generally impossible to make an observation that directly contradicts it or implies a contradiction.

The logical verification of a theory requires that it have logically necessary (or otherwise verifiable) axioms or first principles, and a means of deriving theorems or consequential statements under which truth is heritable. This is what the CTMU, and only the CTMU, brings to the table.

September 16, 2017

57.   Does the CTMU actually predict anything? If so, what? If not, doesn't that disqualify it as not being theorem, (due to the fact that it couldn't be falsifiable)?

Of course the CTMU makes predictions, e.g., the accelerating expansion of the cosmos, the invariance of the speed of light, biological evolution, and so on.

The problem is, so do a number of reverse-engineered theories which, instead of coming at these issues from first principles, proceed from a set of convenient empirically induced assumptions designed to support the "deduction" of such observable facts, often interspersed with similarly back-engineered quantitative equations so that they can pass as "mathematics". These speculative *ad hoc* theories get more airtime than those of independent researchers because their authors are members of Academia, Inc., a sprawling, monopolistic, incredibly profitable intellectual trade organization which promotes its own members ahead of anyone else regardless of minor concerns like truth, honesty, and intelligence.

It seems that once someone pays hundreds of thousand dollars into this glorified trade union and undergoes a bit of circular "peer review" by (*quelle* surprise) other academics, one is as good as gold, gaining automatic respectability for one's supposed "qualifications" to pontificate on one's favorite topics even at the expense of better minds and ideas.

March 20, 2018

Prerequisites

58.   What mathematics is needed to understand Christopher Langan's Cognitive-Theoretic Model of the Universe?

A legitimate question, but first I think we'd better get something straight: there exists no coherent argument to the effect that new theories always require only existing mathematics. Some theories require that one learn new mathematics which are needed for their concise expression. This includes the CTMU, in the source material of which various new mathematical concepts have been introduced.

As for the existing fields of mathematics with which one should have a bit of familiarity before expecting to get the gist of the CTMU, one should definitely understand a little predicate and propositional logic along with rudimentary model theory and a bit of set theory. One should also know a bit about algebra and language theory. A tad of computation theory wouldn't hurt, and neither would a little calculus. (Later on, you'll need much more than that, but first things first.)

Caution: despite their explicit or implicit claims to the contrary, at least a couple of those who have attempted to answer this question obviously lack even the limited mathematical knowledge I've just mentioned. In particular, answers that come down to "None, because the CTMU doesn't have any real mathematical structure!" are absurd and misleading, and should be disregarded.

April 5, 2018

59. What assumed knowledge does one need in order to understand Chris Langan's CTMU?

The CTMU involves no assumptions whatsoever. It requires just two things that each of us is given from birth: The world, and one's ability to perceive and conceive it.

August 16, 2018

60. How much prerequisite physics knowledge is required to understand the CTMU?

An initial grasp of the theory requires only the most basic knowledge of mainstream physics. This includes a bit of classical mechanics, a little Special and General Relativity, a smattering of (standard) quantum mechanics, some introductory cosmology, and so on.

August 16, 2018

Principles

61. (1) Can Chris Langan explain his CTMU M=R principle? (2) Why is it necessarily true?

(1) Very easily. As explained from the time it was first mentioned, the expression "M=R" expresses the duality (*not* dualism) of internal and external state.

(2) It is necessary as a requirement of intelligibility, without which there is no discernible reality to be scientifically explained.

Some people don't like this principle, claiming that it's not a "real mathematical equation". But it certainly is. The problem is that the contentious little geniuses who reject it understand neither the full range of modern mathematical usage of the "=" sign, nor the perils of showing one's ignorance by criticizing what one fails to understand.

February 15, 2018

62. Why should we believe the three fundamental axioms (MAP, M=R, and MU) of Christopher Langan's Cognitive-Theoretic Model of the Universe (CTMU)?

One should believe these three principles because they are true. They reflect dire ontological necessities including the closure and self-duality of reality, neither of which can be rationally characterized as an "assumption".

February 18, 2018

Resistance towards CTMU

63. Is Chris Langan's CTMU being resisted by people lacking virtue?

Over the years, most of the resistance to the CTMU has been found to emanate from people who:

1. Dislike it because they associate it with God, the very idea of Whom they hate;

2. Misunderstand it because they are ignorant or otherwise mentally limited;

3. Oppose it because they envy or resent its author, whom they regard with jealousy or hostility;

4. Hold it in contempt because it was not authored by a professional academic, whereas they indulge academic snobbery;

5. Reject it because they feel that it threatens them and their opinions and preconceptions;

6. Trivialize it because they are lazy, and it looks too much like work.

In other words, they lack some combination of spiritual awareness, reverence, gratitude, knowledge, intelligence, generosity, benevolence, open-mindedness, humility, courage, self-confidence, initiative, and the desire to learn. And because virtually all of them falsely blame their negativity toward the CTMU on the CTMU itself, they also lack honesty.

So regrettably, it would appear that the answer is yes.

May 20, 2017

Responding to criticism

64.   Chris Langan, why haven't you written your CTMU more broken up in such a way that our thought patterns can follow and understand?

Your evident difficulty in understanding the CTMU suggests that your thought patterns are not sufficiently compatible with CTMU structure to comprehend the simplified accounts of it which already exist. In that case, bringing your patterns of thought into conformance with the CTMU may take a bit more effort on your own part. I'm sure that if you put forth this effort, you'll find it well worth your trouble.

I've written about this before, and I don't want to beat a dead horse. But if intellectual commerce and communication were not dominated by an academic monopoly, the CTMU would have "taken off" a long time ago. By now, there would be a huge amount of expository material available on it. Instead, we have a pile of academics arguing so noisily about their own speculative theories, and so thoroughly dominating the media with their ridiculous disputes, that nothing else can be heard above the din.

If one didn't know better, one might almost surmise that mankind doesn't really want to understand reality or reap the benefits of such understanding, but prefers to praise and pamper its academics like precious lapdogs, sacrificing everything to their insatiable desire for attention and pretensions to intellectual greatness.

In which case, all that one can really say is "good luck with that." ;)

June 22, 2017

65.   When will a relatively known academic openly and publicly criticize specific contents of Christopher Langan's Cognitive-Theoretic Model of the Universe (CTMU), putting his reputation at risk because the CTMU is absolutely true?

It could happen any day, although I wouldn't give you a fig for the academic's chances of making his or her "specific criticisms" stick. As I've pointed out repeatedly, the CTMU is logically unassailable, and this is not subject to spontaneous change.

Incidentally, the last paper published on the CTMU ("An Introduction to Mathematical Metaphysics") has reportedly been downloaded many thousands of times, perhaps even setting some kind of record for the academic journal in which it appeared.

January 11, 2018

66.   Can critics of Christopher Langan's Cognitive-Theoretic Model of the Universe (CTMU) offer specific criticism that identifies which specific aspects of the CTMU are false?

CTMU critics occupy two general categories: those who at least partially understand the CTMU, and those who do not.

Those who understand the first thing about the CTMU realize that by virtue of its structure, its content is invulnerable to attack; their critiques thus tend to focus on presentation and emphasis.

On the other hand, this invulnerability to substantive criticism naturally limits those who *do not* understand the CTMU to various indirect and illogical forms of argumentation including straw man arguments, *ad hominem* polemics, stylistic critiques, and irrational outbursts sometimes including insult, profanity, and outright libel (this can be verified right here on Quora, where one malicious but nonetheless popular anti-CTMU screed stridently declares it to be the manure of two different species of large farm animal).

As for the hypothetical possibility of "specifically identifying false aspects" of the CTMU, it would be irrational to assign it a probability greater than zero.

February 10, 2018

67.   What is wrong with Christopher Langan's Cognitive-Theoretic Model of the Universe (CTMU)?

Absolutely nothing ... nothing at all.

In order to make sense of this question, it must be modified to read:

"What has gone wrong with the communication of the CTMU?"

This form of the question is very easy to answer. Every communication process involves a sender, a receiver, and a channel, and all three must be functioning properly for the message to be properly communicated. Unfortunately, only one of these three components has been functioning properly with respect to the CTMU communication process: the sender.

As for the other two components, the channel is not functioning properly because it is under the monopolistic control of Academia, Inc., which denies full access to anyone lacking its certification, and most of those at the receiving end of the transmission are too disinterested and/or intellectually impaired to comprehend the message even when they manage to hear it.

Should any professional academic with a reputation to protect want to take issue with this, he or she is welcome to try. I'll be frank: there is no professional academic on this planet who is even remotely knowledgeable enough to attack the CTMU in the full light of day and avoid being crushed by me.

(This offer applies only to known figures who are both reputable and well-qualified in fields related to the CTMU. For others, the penalty for specious argumentation is insufficient to "keep them honest", so to speak. They stand to gain too much more than they risk by engaging with known figures, and are too likely to engage in specious argumentation and dirty polemics.)

[**Note 1**: Another answer for this question, evidently with comments disabled, criticizes the CTMU on the alleged grounds that "a panentheistic god is outside of time and space, somewhat like the Abrahamic God, thus beyond reality and not merely generated by reality." This is mistaken. A panentheistic God, being metaphysical, properly includes physical reality and is thus omnipresent therein. The CTMU is precisely what it takes to fully realize this criterion.]

[**Note 2**: Yet another answer is followed by comments from one "David Moore" (again with replies disabled), who criticizes the CTMU on the alleged grounds that "educe" means "infer", and that the CTMU therefore runs afoul of Godel's theorems. In fact, the first definition of "educe" is "to bring out or develop", which is consistent with undecidability. Mr. Moore also states that "tautologies imply nothing except themselves...". However, while this is superficially true for *propositional* tautologies, tautology is in fact a much more general concept, and the CTMU applies it in a whole new way.]

February 24, 2018

68. What do other profoundly gifted individuals think of Christopher Langan's Cognitive-Theoretic Model of the Universe (CTMU)?

To my knowledge, no profoundly gifted individual has ever found fault with the CTMU. No *real, verified* one, that is.

As for the nasty answers posted here, I'm afraid they're more likely to have come from resentful mediocrities than "profoundly gifted individuals". I've been dealing with the profoundly gifted for decades, and none of these people sounds anything like them.

August 15, 2018

69. Why do people claim that the conclusions of the CTMU are "unjustified assertions" when they are all results of rigorous deductions (including logical induction)?

There are several possible reasons. E.g., they don't like theories said to be related to God; they don't like people who are said to be smarter than they are; they don't like theories related to God and written by people who are smarter than they are, and so on.

But perhaps the most important reason is that of those who claim to understand logic, few actually do. They merely *pretend* to understand logic, and in order to console themselves for their ignorance of logic, use their misunderstandings of logic to attack theories about which they have yet other misunderstandings.

In short, it's all one big misunderstanding. ;)

August 21, 2018

70.   Why does Chris Langan receive so much unreasonable hostility from otherwise reasonable people just for saying what he thinks like everyone else does? Is it that people are threatened by his high IQ, causing them to feel a need to assert themselves?

Permission to speak frankly? It's because, when one is just a cheesy, resentful, pseudonymous little Internet troll with a hard-on for God, the CTMU, and anyone reputed to be more intelligent than oneself, one has nothing of value to lose by shooting off one's vile, foaming mouth like a messy, smelly vinegar-and-baking soda Vesuvius whenever one gets the chance.

August 28, 2018

Scientists and CTMU

71.   What do scientists think of Chris Langan's CTMU?

There are two kinds of science: empirical, and logico-mathematical or linguistic (logic and mathematics are just special kinds of language). They are inseparable in the sense that while mathematics exists in the minds of observable (physical) entities including mathematicians, the theoretical aspect of empirical science is dependent on logic and mathematics along with other ingredients of language.

In order to deal with the mutual dependency relationship between mathematical and observational reality, we require a level of science which spans both. This is the sense in which the CTMU is "scientific"; it is science of a higher and more powerful kind than empirical or mathematical science alone. In the vast majority of cases, neither mathematical nor empirical scientists are properly trained for this level of scientific discourse.

Model theory is a branch of logic having to do with the interpretation of empirical phenomena in theories and the mathematical structures of which they consist. Technically, the CTMU is a special kind of model theory designed to support the description of reality on the ontological level of discourse ... the level on which reality fundamentally "exists". On this level of science, the CTMU is absolutely impervious to attack. Just as logic itself contains no assumptions, neither does the CTMU. No one has ever gotten to first base against it, and no one ever will.

While many scientists have been misled into believing that their academic training should allow them to understand and even pass judgment on a high-level scientific theory like the CTMU, nothing could be farther from the truth. Nevertheless, some of the more incautious among them – especially those who fear its apparent theological implications – have expressed extremely negative opinions of it and its author (me). It is important to remember that none of these people has ever succeeded in putting a dent in it, and that every one of them could be easily crushed by anyone with sufficient understanding.

Readers are advised to bear this in mind as they read some of the other answers in this thread.

May 12, 2017

Syntax and state

72. What do "syntax" and "state" mean in Christopher Langan's Cognitive-Theoretic Model of the Universe (CTMU)?

In the CTMU, these terms refer to properties and valuations thereof.

[Please note: The level of detail in my answers regarding the CTMU, which was authored by me around three decades ago, is being limited by the apparent efforts of another Quora participant to appropriate them. In particular, Quora seems to have become a major outlet for a self-described 22 year-old philosophy undergraduate who is trying to put together a graduate thesis, and is apparently bent on doing it by feigning originality for certain aspects of my work. Although he already claims to have a "more elegant, precise and complete" "theory of metaphysics" which he tries to pass off as "naturalistic" (a contradiction in terms), I have seen no evidence whatsoever of scientific, mathematical, or philosophical competence in anything he has written. This person's constant efforts to misinform people about the CTMU are harmful to the veracity of Quora. Thanks for your attention.]

February 14, 2018

Understanding the importance of CTMU

73.   Do people realize how important it is to understand the CTMU and save billions of souls and for the sake of one's neighbor to truly change the course of mankind which is only possible with a new worldview and not with more technology?

Some do and some don't.

To some, a theory must be "useful" in order to be worthwhile, and no theory is "useful" which does not immediately lead to the manufacture of one or more physical substances or devices to satisfy their material needs or serve their convenience, amusement, or pleasure.

Obviously, these people are incapable of forming meaningful judgments regarding theories of which the primary (explicit) applications are psychological, social, political, spiritual, or comparable. Give them a theory with the potential to reveal man's inner nature, bring people together, and save the world, and they'll simply complain, in effect, that it cannot be eaten, worn, driven, or used to play videos and send email.

On the other hand, some people rationally admit that human utility exists in non-commercial areas as well as commercial ones, and display a refreshing measure of intellectual competence in recognizing the characteristics that a viable worldview or ideology must exhibit. It is these people among whom the CTMU finds its most ardent and discerning followers, and not unrelatedly, on whose shoulders the fate of humanity rests.

(Of course, this is not to be construed to mean that the CTMU lacks scientific and technological applications. But the clear existence of psychological, social, political, spiritual, and other cognitive or "anthropic" applications suffice for the dismissal of those who irrationally deny their importance.)

February 5, 2018

Uniqueness

74. What is the world's current, in use, equivalent to Christopher Langan's Cognitive-Theoretic Model of the Universe (CTMU)?

The CTMU is unique, and has the conceptual structure to prove it. In fact, it can be described as an ontological characterization of self-uniqueness, and as such, it occupies a higher level of discourse than any other human conceptual framework.

However, with certain exceptions which vary from example to example, the best mainstream approximations of the CTMU might include (1) certain strains of advanced mainstream mathematics, particularly at the foundational level; (2) certain novel scientific constructs like the Holographic Universe; (3) certain works of mainstream philosophy like A.N. Whitehead's "panentheism"; and (4) the world's great religions, each of which instantiates certain aspects of it.

Bear in mind that none of these examples "duplicates" the CTMU to any large extent, and that all include statements that must be modified or eliminated for complete CTMU consistency (if only as doctrinal baggage). The CTMU accepts none of them *a priori*, and brings to bear certain insights that all of them lack.

February 1, 2018

DM THEORY

Acutt, Matt

75. Matt Acutt seems to understand Christopher Langan's Cognitive-Theoretic Model of the Universe (CTMU) well enough to criticize it. Can he explain what exactly are its fundamental assumptions, possibly in common English, thus making the theory unsound?

I'm the author of the CTMU.

On the basis of the limited material we've seen from Mr. Acutt regarding his aptly-named (DMT) "theory", I do not accept the premise that he "understands the CTMU well enough to criticize it" effectively. It seems to me that where he does not simply misunderstand what the CTMU actually says, he argues in favor of the illogical or logically untenable.

If Mr. Acutt's CTMU comprehension ever improves to a level at which I find that his concerns make sense to me, I may decide to address them. Meanwhile, I would merely observe that anyone who wants to initiate a debate on philosophy should choose a topic of which one has a thorough understanding.

As a general rule, I have more pressing things to do with my time than serve as an unpaid CTMU tutor for self-styled metaphysicians who criticize my work even when they exhibit little or no understanding of it.

Thank you for your attention.

January 9, 2018

DMT vs CTMU

76.   Is Chris Langan's CTMU superior to Matt Acutt's DMT?

Yes, vastly. The CTMU is an exact, original, and tightly integrated theory of mathematical metaphysics introduced by me in the 1980's and mentioned by numerous sources in the mainstream media. Due to certain unique properties, it is demonstrably superior to any other theory of metaphysics.

In contrast, "DMTheory", as it is somewhat comically named (note the unwitting double-entendre), is a jumbled hodgepodge of disconnected pieces – some from the CTMU itself – which has been slapped together by some number of absurdly ambitious college undergraduates with nothing better to do, and presented here on Quora as though there were something to it. My best guess is that these kids are shooting for the position of "world's foremost naturalistic metaphysicians" (an oxymoron), buoyed to fame and fortune by their virulent opposition to the CTMU. One almost admires their cheek. But while it never looks good to take candy from babies, their bubble begs to be popped ... if only to spare Quora readers from being inundated with philosophical misinformation.

[Note (from the Comments): The problem with "DMTheory" is very easy to state. Naturalism says that everything arises from natural objects, properties, and causes – i.e., from nature, which in the broadest sense is the physical or material world or universe (Wikipedia) – with no metaphysical, supernatural, or spiritual explanation required. This means unequivocally that "naturalistic metaphysics" comes down to "physicalistic or materialistic metaphysics", which is an oxymoron plain and simple. This oxymoron is the very starting point of "DMTheory", which purportedly combines physical data with "logic" while excluding any ontological support for the latter due to its non-physicality. This means that "DMTheory" is pure nonsense, and that discussing it is a complete waste of everybody's time. (Note also that I've just deleted an incoherent attempt to justify this nonsense using "the metaverse" along with yet more nonsense including "absolute materialism". Pardon me, but I've had it with this garbage – at worst it's gobbledygook, and at best it's just a CTMU rip-off undertaken thirty years too late.)]

February 21, 2018

77.   Which is correct: DataLogical Metaphysical Theory or Christopher Langan's Cognitive-Theoretic Model of the Universe (CTMU)?

The CTMU is a theory of mathematical metaphysics with a unique logical structure which ensures its correctness. It has had this structure ever since it was conceived decades ago, before the promoters of "DataLogical Metaphysical Theory" were born.

The CTMU is tight and technically precise. It has been published in several academic journals. It has been mentioned on several major news networks and is known to hundreds of thousands if not millions of people throughout the world. It has profound applications from science and mathematics to philosophy and theology. Its unique mathematical structure is duplicated by no other theory in existence, including "DataLogical Metaphysical Theory" (the promoters of which are evidently incapable of understanding it, given their confused, irrelevant, incessant CTMU critiques here on Quora). Its only problem, in fact, is being a magnet for ignorant and obsessive trolls, who are seemingly drawn to it as flies to honey.

As for "DMTheory", this is from my answer to a previous similar question here on Quora (of which there have been several):

"DMTheory", as it is somewhat comically named (note the unwitting double-entendre), is a jumbled hodgepodge of disconnected pieces – some from the CTMU itself – which has been slapped together by some number of absurdly ambitious college undergraduates with nothing better to do, and presented here on Quora as though there were something to it. My best guess is that these kids are shooting for the position of "world's foremost naturalistic metaphysicians" (an oxymoron), buoyed to fame and fortune by their virulent opposition to the CTMU. One almost admires their cheek. But while it never looks good to take candy from babies, their bubble begs to be popped … if only to spare Quora readers from being inundated with philosophical misinformation.

The problem with "DMTheory" is very easy to state. Naturalism says that everything arises from natural objects, properties, and causes – i.e., from *nature*, which in the broadest sense is the physical or material world or universe (Wikipedia) – with no metaphysical, supernatural, or spiritual explanation required. This means unequivocally that "naturalistic metaphysics" comes down to "physicalistic or materialistic metaphysics", which is an oxymoron plain and simple. This oxymoron is the very starting point of "DMTheory", which purportedly combines physical data with "logic" while excluding any ontological support for the latter due to its non-physicality. This means that "DMTheory" is pure nonsense, and that discussing it is a complete waste of everybody's time.

March 2, 2018

ETHICS

Christian morality

78.   What does Christopher Langan think about Christian morality?

I embrace it. However, it must be noted that as most people understand it, "Christian morality" is in some ways a rather ill-defined concept. While I agree with morality based on the underlying logic of the Golden Rule and the rest of the New Testament, many sectarian versions of so-called "Christian morality" are based on nonlogical interpretations of Christian scripture associated with various bodies of doctrine authored long after the New Testament was written. Just as Christian scripture is independent of sectarian doctrine, so is the morality which can be directly derived from it on a purely logical basis.

March 11, 2018

Ethical system and abortion

79.   Would the existence of artificial wombs change the abortion debate?

Not really. Without a verifiable set of ethical principles covering this issue (and other abortion-related issues), such questions qualify as little more than baseless opinion magnets. A valid ethical system covering all aspects of abortion would have to be sociobiologically parameterized, and could not avoid the reasoned consideration of eugenics ("genetic hygiene", in the socially and biologically rational sense of the concept). Unfortunately, this is diametrically opposed by "political correctness".

May 12, 2017

Eugenics as genetic hygiene

80.   Is Chris Langan a racist by implication or otherwise of his support for eugenics?

This question seems to come down to "Does support for eugenics (under its original and valid definition) imply racism?"

The answer is very clear: NO. Eugenics, defined as the maintenance or improvement of human genetic quality and integrity, can be pursued without respect to race, or even simultaneously within each existing racial group.

However, there seem to be some unspoken assumptions here ... for example, that Christopher Langan is a "eugenicist" under some unspecified definition of the term. Where the definition is allowed to vary, the accuracy of this assumption would depend on the particular definition that is chosen.

For example, where eugenics is defined as reasonable attention to genetic hygiene in order to prevent genomic degradation and reverse evolution attending the artificial suspension of environmental constraints and limitations – i.e., the suspension of "natural selection" using medical and other kinds of technology – the assumption would be accurate. (Show me someone who does not share this opinion, and I'll show you someone who is profoundly irrational on the species level of human identity.)

But where eugenics describes the current effort of the parasitic oligarchy to monopolize adaptive traits by "dumbing down", suicidally indoctrinating, and genetically homogenizing various sectors of the human population without respect to fitness (as defined with respect to a sustainable refinement of modern civilization), the assumption would be false. In particular, I am against the use of weaponized mass immigration to commit demographic genocide against the indigenous populations of all and only Western (White majority) nations, as well as the rapid ongoing destruction of Western culture, family values, educational integrity, population genetics, and patterns of reproduction in the name of multiculturalism, diversity, and social justice.

[There is an answer below which accuses me of wanting to "sterilize people with low IQs, average IQs, *and* moderately high IQs", and even to drag young girls away from their parents in order to perform "invasive surgical procedures" on them. Nowhere have I ever advocated anything of the kind. The answer in question is factually incorrect, misleading, and defamatory.]

January 11, 2018

FACEBOOK

Discussion group

81.   Does Chris Langan read the CTMU FB Discussion page?

I've visited the page only a couple of times. But then again, I just managed to get subscribed. (Please bear in mind that if I were to answer every question that anyone feels like asking me, I'd get very little done on the CTMU *or* the ranch. The US economy is degenerate, and good help is getting very hard to find these days. You can't even find a high school kid willing to mow the lawn – apparently, most of them are either lazy or get too much allowance. Or maybe it's that they're "above all that", being precious snowflakes who prefer to reserve their time for the properly vetted PC/ SJW campaigns of their choosing.)

UPDATE (June 03, 2017): A very queer situation has arisen at Facebook, apparently due to policies instituted by its proprietor Mark Zuckerberg. Although I'm given to understand that Facebook has several accounts for "Christopher Langan" and even "Christopher Michael Langan", the *real* "Christopher Michael Langan", namely yours truly, was recently delisted from Facebook on the absurd premise, advanced by an obvious troll, that I was "using a false identity" (the name under which I've gone since I was 6 years old) to contribute to the Facebook CTMU Group. In short, all the fake and/or lesser-known "Christopher Langans" are still on Facebook; only the real one, from whom people really want to hear, has been rejected.

Naturally, I appealed this decision, sending in two (2) forms of identification listed in the Facebook document "What types of ID does Facebook accept?" Breaking its own rules, Facebook declined to restore my account! I hate to have to say it, but it seems that Facebook rules are strictly for those with whom Mark Zuckerberg, a notorious atheist, happens to agree. Unfortunately, Christopher Michael Langan does not appear to be a person with whom Mr. Zuckerberg agrees.

As long-time CTMU fans are well aware, the CTMU and I have been subject to vicious attack by atheistic trolls for the last three decades. This is just the most recent proof that there is something concerted, coherent, and to put it bluntly, nasty and counterproductive going on with the "New Atheism" (i.e., the Old Atheism dressed up in the emperor's new clothing) ... which is why, for example, there is no CTMU article on Wikipedia to this very day.

It's been dirty pool all the way with CTMU/Langan critics in the social media. It's the only kind of pool these people seem to know.

June 3, 2017

FREE WILL

Free will vs predestination

82. How does Christopher Langan's Cognitive-Theoretic Model of the Universe (CTMU) resolve the conflict between predestination and free will?

By simultaneously and consistently interpreting both of the concepts "free will" and "predestination" in the structure of the CTMU. (In any other conceptual setting, these concepts are too ill-defined to conflict as usually assumed; when properly defined and interpreted in the CTMU, they do not conflict.)

February 26, 2018

Humans as telors

83. Can Chris Langan prove that free will exists?

Yes, I can. It's a matter of properly characterizing the freedom of reality itself, and then showing that this freedom is internally replicated for systems meeting the appropriate criteria *within* reality (in the CTMU, these special subsystems of reality are called *telors*).

Such a proof is possible only within the CTMU. Others have advanced their own arguments for free will, or pointed to what they assume is "evidence" for free will. However, the arguments and evidence in question are selectively interpreted in light of supporting assumptions which are themselves both ill-defined and devoid of any proof whatsoever. As the CTMU requires no assumptions, it avoids this shortcoming.

In principle, human beings are telors and therefore possess free will. However, many are degenerate, having surrendered or sold their freedom in return for various amenities and necessities of survival. This is largely why the world often seems to be hurtling toward self-destruction like a runaway freight train.

February 13, 2018

Meaning of life

84.   Does Chris Langan believe in free will?

Yes. My belief in free will stems from my knowledge concerning it. This knowledge relates to a theory of mathematical metaphysics called the **CTMU (Cognitive Theoretic Model of the Universe)**. The CTMU is the only intrinsically viable, self-contained ontology in existence. In fact, it is the only one possible.

[Note: Another answer to this question, emanating from a troll account of which Quora Moderation has been repeatedly informed but to no avail, asserts that free will is pointless if there are penalties attached to its improper use. However, the point of free will is not to use it improperly, but to use it properly in service of teleology, thus avoiding the metaphysical penalties attached to its chronic abuse. One is allowed to make the occasional honest mistake, but not to latch onto the same tired mistake over and over again like a mad dog, growling and gnawing and foaming from the mouth. (Free will is a requisite of meaning in our lives, but can be a very dangerous thing. It's a pass-fail test of sorts, but with very appreciable risks and rewards attached to one's score. Obviously, it is best that everyone understand this, and not end up having to whine about it as though one had no choice between good and evil.)]

June 23, 2018

GOD

Conformance to logic

85.   God is who He says He is. He created the universe and us. What right do we have to expect Him to conform to our ideas of who He is or should be?

We may expect God to conform to our ideas of Who and What God should be precisely when they have achieved cognitive emergence in logical form, thus reversing the mapping by which God originally implanted them in the human mind. (Despite its concision and explicit invocation of logic, this answer is fully consistent with the New Testament and compatible scriptures.)

In other words, God does indeed tell us Who and What He is, and He does it with logic, which provides the only general means of verifying the message. This convergence of theological information and verification is no accident; unverifiable theological information is ultimately pointless, and God always has a point.

Obviously, any denial of what God tells us with logic is trivially false, and the deniers are illogical by definition. Such people and their opinions may be safely ignored for theological purposes.

May 9, 2017

Defining God

86. What is God according to Chris Langan? What does he think about the established religions such as Christianity or Islam?

God, best understood as Ultimate Reality, has (supertautological) structure which implies certain properties which are consistent with the definitions of God that occur in major world religions like Christianity, Islam, and Judaism.

Simultaneously modeling the main scriptural components of these religions in this structure makes them theologically and ontologically consistent.

Theological and ontological consistency is limited to just those religions which can be modeled in this way.

January 12, 2018

Endomorphic images

87. In the CTMU, human beings are seen as endomorphic images of the mind of God. Can this mapping be described? We are very constrained local entities, so how does it work?

In the CTMU, the global identity of reality is explicitly stratified, and distributed morphisms are utilized. So (1) one needs to be very clear on the level of identity to which any given statement or mathematical symbol refers, and (2) one needs to allow for the distributed nature of certain morphisms, where by *distributed* we mean that the morphism applies to *each point* in a topological point set.

Notice the implication: the use of distributed morphisms implies that each point of any topological space subject to distributed morphism has internal structure. In the CTMU, this internal structure is called *syntax*; hence, the points are called *syntactic operators*.

Some syntactic operators cannot support full isomorphism to the global identity; hence, they are subject to syntactic restriction, and isomorphism is limited to some proper part or aspect of global syntax. But the points in which the syntax of the global identity is *fully* imaged are not restricted in this way. It follows that their syntax is isomorphic to global syntax. (This does *not* imply isomorphism with respect to external state.)

And now for a bit of advice. Typically, questions like this come from people who have not bothered to read available material on the CTMU. They are looking for fast answers, they are often confused, and many of them dislike work so much that they don't even review the answers I've already posted on Quora. Unfortunately, this gives others the opportunity to post false or misleading answers, and Quora is sometimes very lax in letting such people misinform its readers.

Readers are therefore cautioned against blindly accepting any answer for any CTMU question on its face unless it comes from me or someone else whose knowledge of the theory can be verified by checking it against the available material, especially if it emanates from someone who has been guilty of misinterpreting and/or badmouthing the CTMU in the past.

September 28, 2018

Logical theology

88. What is logical theology? How does it relate to Chris Langan and the CTMU?

Logical theology consists of the theological (God-related) implications of the CTMU, a metaphysical formulation of logic.

Others have used this term to describe strains of theology that conform to their ideas of logic. However, (1) "ideas of logic" often deviate from any well-defined logico-mathematical structure known to logicians and mathematicians; (2) it is hard to derive theological implications from standard logic; and (3) problems arise when trying to employ standard logic on the metaphysical level of discourse required by theology.

Properly applied to theology, the CTMU solves problems 1–3.

May 23, 2018

Omnipotence

89.   Do you accept that any god could not be omnipotent due to the
       logical paradoxes this creates?

In order to infer divine non-omnipotence from, for example, the paradoxical assertion that an omnipotent God could create a rock too heavy for
God to lift, one must be able to show that God Himself is not responsible
for the operative constraints on His power, as these take precedence
over God's self-imposed "inability" to lift the rock.

In other words, if God has tied His own hands by establishing prior
constraints or commitments that prevent Him from lifting a given rock
(or doing anything else), then the real measure of His power is the establishment of these prior constraints, and the real measure of His will is
His own refusal to break them.

Human examples are easy to find. E.g., it would be misleading and ridiculous to accuse a smoker who successfully forbids himself to smoke one
more cigarette of "lacking willpower". In fact, willpower is exactly what
such a person demonstrates.

As long as God Himself is responsible for any limitations on His own
power, including even the structure of logic, this remains entirely
consistent with divine omnipotence.

August 15, 2018

Proving God's existence

90.   Why is the physical world the best proof of God?

If you're talking about the physical world alone, it is not the "best proof"
of the existence of God. The reason is very simple but often overlooked:
proof is a two-way street with a sender on one end and receivers on
the other, and many receivers are defective. In particular, those who
disbelieve in God typically attribute the physical world to a cosmogonic
form of "randomness" (with respect to origination) and cite "logic" as
their pretext for rejecting any claim to the contrary. They can receive
no information through this blockage.

The physical world is indeed the (partial) basis of proof, but must be combined with logic and mathematics to constitute a proof that defeats the fake, hand-waving sort of "logic" brought to bear against it by atheists and materialists.

[date unknown]

91. Can Christopher Langan's Cognitive-Theoretic Model of the Universe (CTMU) prove God's existence by logic?

The answer is *yes*, and it is completely unequivocal. This is obviously not the forum in which to argue about it, as out of the 10 answers which have thus far been posted, at least 8 are saying *no* for entirely the wrong reasons.

If you want a meaningful debate about this, my advice would be to find a widely recognized authority on the subject and get him to express an opinion on the matter under his real name in the full light of day, with his reputation on the line just as mine is. That way, he or she has something to lose as well as something to gain, and I have something to gain as well as something to lose (that's how fair debates are conducted).

Examples: Richie Dawkins, Daniel Dennett, Sam Harris, or someone else of that ilk. (Your problem, of course, will be that these people have been ducking me for years, and don't want me to publicly mop the floor with them. Which I can certainly do.)

May 7, 2017

92. How does Christopher Langan's Cognitive-Theoretic Model of the Universe (CTMU) prove the existence of a god?

The CTMU proves the existence of God by (1) explicating the deep structure of reality, and (2) showing that this structure possesses attributes conventionally ascribed to God.

No qualified and well-reputed physicist, philosopher, mathematician, linguist, theologian, or other professional has ever demonstrated that the CTMU contains a single error, or that it is not what I've just said it is, or that it fails to do what I've just said it does. In all likelihood, at least part of the reason for this is that no qualified, well-reputed professional academic in any relevant field is intellectually capable of doing so and making it stick, at least under his or her real name in the full light of day.

After nearly 30 years since the first papers were published on this subject, sincere and well-motivated readers may consider the CTMU and its implications to be written in stone. Further clarifications will be forthcoming.

(Papers on the CTMU have, by the way, been published in peer-reviewed journals. It is hard to say why any CTMU critic would deny this. But two fairly obvious reasons are that the critic recognizes only a select subset of journals in specific fields – in a word, "academic snobbery" – or that the critic is simply trying to conceal his or her inability to understand the content, in which case he or she should not be making negative comments about it on social media sites.)

May 11, 2017

93.   Would an atheist believe in God if he/she found proofs beyond a doubt of God's existence?

No, and the reason is very clear: disbelief is a cognitive filter. In order to recognize a proof of the existence of God, one's mind must be open to the possibility, and true atheists have closed their minds to any such intellectual content. Thus, they cannot "find" (or recognize) such a proof in the first place.

I have thirty years of relatively high-profile experience with this. The minds of most atheists are cognitive wind-up toys which absolutely cannot be swayed by any theory, model, or form of reasoning which even smells like it might confute their (anti)theological preconceptions. Wind them up by mentioning the possible existence of God, and their minds instantly spiral into an infinite loop.

The underlying conceptual mechanics are also very clear. Real atheists (as opposed to so-called "agnostic atheists" or agnostics with mere atheistic leanings) implicitly or explicitly subscribe to "metaphysical naturalism", a self-reinforcing (and therefore academically dominant) worldview which oxymoronically excludes the metaphysical from its arbitrary physicalistic conception of reality and thus precludes any meaningful (metaphysical) definition of God. Obviously, the existence of X cannot be proven to anyone who refuses to let X be properly defined.

So you see, reasoning with true atheists on this matter is simply not in the cards. The only "atheist" who could possibly be convinced of the existence of God is one who unwittingly falls somewhere short of true atheism.

July 19, 2017

94.   Is God really there? How can you prove it?

Proof is a logical operation. It follows that there is just one way to prove the existence of God: using logic. Unfortunately, the things with which standard logic ordinarily deals do not include God, Who resists being captured by it (because, in effect, God is by definition the One Who spans all that exists and thus does all the "capturing"). Therefore, logic must be adapted to the task in question, and reformulated on the metaphysical level of discourse. Proving the existence of God thus requires a system called the CTMU, which incorporates the required metaphysical formulation of logic.

[date unknown]

95.   How does CTMU prove that God exists?

The CTMU proves that God exists by providing a valid framework for the overall structure of reality, and showing that this structure exhibits properties traditionally attributed to God.

Note: I see that someone is requesting a definition of God. In the CTMU, God is defined as *Ultimate Reality*, with a recursive base consisting of *perceptual reality* (the physical world) plus its regularities (patterns). "Ultimate" means, roughly, "idempotent with respect to containment and explanation". This has been the CTMU definition of God for decades.

(Those with questions about the theory might try reading up a little, especially if you're capable of handling appreciable abstraction – abstraction is the name of the game when it comes to metaphysical reasoning.

It may be hard to believe, but some people really can't handle much of it at all. This evidently includes many people who use Quora, even some who claim to respect "science".)

July 11, 2018

96.   Is it possible to use science to prove or disprove the existence of God?

There are two kinds of science: mathematical and empirical.

The only statements that can be proven in the empirical sciences are (1) observation statements about things that can be directly observed with replication; and (2) statements that can be logically deduced from replicable observation statements.

Where *God* is defined as *omnipresent*, He cannot be directly observed in His entirety; and because nothing that is not omnipresent qualifies as God, God's existence cannot be empirically verified using limited powers of observation. Because our powers of observation are limited not only by the cosmic horizon, but by the limits of quantum measurement expressed in terms of Heisenberg uncertainty, God's presence goes beyond our observational limitations on the macroscopic and microscopic scales; His extent exceeds our ability to perceive it. Due to Hume's Problem of Induction, which is related to the horizon and uncertainty problems, His existence cannot be logically deduced from limited observation statements alone.

This rules out the empirical sciences, leaving only the mathematical sciences to consider. But here we arrive at another set of problems, including the form of dualism whereby statements deduced from mathematical axioms cannot be globally attributed to any incompletely observable external universe to which those axioms might hypothetically apply. Again, the problem of induction rears its head; that the axioms of a theoretical language are found to apply in any given region of its universe does not mean that they necessarily apply everywhere.

It turns out that what is actually required is a higher-level proof system capable of generically relating theories, their universes, and their model-theoretic relationships, and thus of uniting the mathematical and empirical sciences. Called a "metaformal system", it has a unique structure that was explicated decades ago as the CTMU, short for *Cognitive Theoretic Model of the Universe.*

In other words, this is a well-solved problem, and has been for quite some time. If one likes, one can simply forget about the dozens of conjectural answers to this question and concentrate on this one alone. On the other hand, anyone who is unable to understand what I've just written, or doesn't like the conclusions to which my answer leads – e.g., "God exists" – is free to keep on groping.

May 3, 2018

97. Is Chris Langan's CTMU the first intellectual production to incontrovertibly prove God's existence? Didn't any earlier philosophers (e.g. Kant, Hegel) make cogent cases before him?

While many well-known philosophers have attempted, over the centuries, to "make cogent cases" for the existence of God, they all lacked a coherent and comprehensive metaphysical framework in which to do so.

As the CTMU is inarguably the required metaphysical framework, it alone can support the rehabilitation or restructuring of their arguments and carry the issue to its proper conclusion.

June 13, 2018

98. How can I explain the CTMU, the proof of God and the afterlife with metaphysical logic, to an atheist?

Science and human experience depend on the intelligibility of what science studies, and what people experience. This means that the integrity of science depends on an explanation for the intelligibility of physical reality.

The CTMU is a high-level formulation of logic designed to provide such an explanation. It answers questions like the following: What is it that makes reality identifiable? What features does reality possess that make science and human experience possible – what forms do they assume in the overall structure of the cosmos? How do these features manifest on all scales?

The nonoccurrence of irresolvable paradox in physical reality is a scientific fact. No scientist has ever managed to observe an irresolvable paradox; somehow, reality maintains its consistency under all circumstances. When a scientist sees what looks like an inconsistency in the structure of reality, the usual paradox-avoidance strategy is simply to make the paradox vanish by adjusting an existing theory, or finding a new one. *But why should this work?*

The undeniable fact is that science has no answers for questions like these, and mainstream philosophy has been of no help. Science lacks any cognitive framework in which the actual relationship between theory and content, knowledge and reality, epistemology and ontology, can be expressed, and its standard methodology does not permit this deficiency to be meaningfully addressed. In order to remedy this situation, it must be shown how and why reality is able to maintain its self-consistency and ontological integrity. This is what the CTMU does, *and more*.

I've scanned some of the answers below. Most are full of ignorance and derision, contain almost zero information on the CTMU, and are profoundly misleading. Readers are hereby advised to be on guard against the efforts of Quora's ever-expanding troll population to mislead the unwary about a theory that its members, for all intents and purposes, are intellectually incapable of understanding. That a few of these people seem to know a smattering of scientific and/or philosophical terminology is beside the point, as they evidently have no idea how to properly apply it.

[The other parts of this question, which is actually several questions in one, are addressed in other answers I've posted on this site. A bit less misinformation out of you trolls, please.]

July 21, 2018

99.   Can the CTMU prove God with roughly 80 symbols?

Of course, and easily. However, the definitions of those symbols might exceed that number, and even the term "symbol" might not be defined in quite the usual way.

August 21, 2018

Self-configuration

100.   What created God according to Chris Langan?

God is eternal. He exists without respect to any external clock; clocks exist *within* God, not outside of him (basically, that's why time is relative in General Relativity; this relates to something called "background free-dom", specifically from any external standard or metric). On His most general level of Being, God simply *exists*. All change in or evolution of the structure of God, known in the CTMU as "Self-configuration" (often through secondary telors), is strictly internal to God Himself.

February 28, 2018

Self-integrity

101. Does Rabbi Harold Kushner correctly imply that God cannot violate physics because God invented physics, and God does not destroy his creations usually?

Yes, given a sufficiently broad definition of "physics" which recognizes its necessary embedment in metaphysics. (With this qualification, the Rabbi is not the only one to have acknowledged such an implication.)

On the global level of nomological invariance, God does not break His own laws, for this would be to paradoxically violate His own will. The law that reality does not contain irresolvable paradoxes is certainly inviolable, as any violation would render reality self-inconsistent and therefore unintelligible, when in fact, we know reality to be intelligible by our very ability to identify it through direct observation with mutual perceptual corroboration.

The problem is to determine the exact form of the invariants that God, defined as the Ultimate Reality, must preserve for the sake of His own Self-integrity. It is important to note that these are not necessarily "laws of physics" as *physics* is ordinarily understood.

Fortunately, there is a *metaphysical* theory which permits such determinations, namely, the Cognitive Theoretic Model of the Universe (CTMU).

[**Note**: The original form of this question was "Does (−) correctly imply that God cannot violate physics because God invented physics?" As for the part which has been added to the original question, I do not necessarily agree that God "usually does not destroy His creations". He destroys them, with nonviolation of high-level Self-consistency, precisely when they persistently fail to serve His purposes, with the understanding that on the level of metaphysical invariance, His purposes are *always* served.]

October 21, 2017

Ultimate Reality

102. Is God ultimate reality?

Yes, beyond any shadow of doubt.

This answer can be logically justified with complete certainty in a unique "metamodel" of reality called the CTMU. It can be gainsaid by no other belief system (including Zen and other forms of Buddhism), as the CTMU is a reflexive model-theoretic extension of logic in which every intelligible belief system is by definition embedded, and which is as inviolable as predicate and propositional logic themselves. (Note that *sunyata*, whether regarded as an ontological feature of reality, a meditation state, or a phenomenological analysis of experience, has conceptual structure and is therefore subject to the demands of logic.)

In short, just as there can be no escape from ultimate reality, there can be no escape from God. Make peace with Him, or pay the price: dissolution and reabsorption, not necessarily without a very great deal of pain and regret in the "dissolution" phase (as deserved).

Good luck on the road to enlightenment regarding the true nature of being.

February 13, 2018

Worshipping God

103. How can it be wrong to worship God in other forms?

Not to worship God in totality is in effect to deny some aspects of God, which amounts to denying God, period.

October 31, 2017

INFOCOGNITION

Definition

104. What is the definition of "infocognition" by Chris Langan?

Infocognition is a convergent generalization of information and cognition based on the fact that *cognition* is a process which, by definition, *informs* (generates *information* for) the cognitive processor.

That is, when you (let's call you "X") cognitively apprehend Y, you are *informed of* Y by the act of cognition. Conversely, when anything X is *informed of* (or affected by) something Y which causes a state transition in X, this amounts to what can be described as a *generalized cognition* event, namely the (re)cognition of Y by X.

Thus, by the universality of information, it is possible to generalize cognition in such a way that the coupling is universal.

January 13, 2018

INTELLIGENCE

Brain

105. How is a person's brain with a high IQ physically different from a person with a low IQ?

Well, I suppose I'm the highest-profile living specimen with relevance to this question, having been mentioned in this regard by multiple sources in the mass media.

My cranial volume, computed by subjecting *in vivo* caliper measurements to several estimation formulae including the Lee-Pearson formula and the spheroid formula, is in the neighborhood of 50 percent greater than that of the average human male, almost enough to be considered a species-level difference. (I'd be considered large-framed, but I'm really not far above the human average in this regard.)

Not too much should be made of this, as there are many other morphological, physiological, and especially neurological criteria to consider. However, one of them is *not* environment – my brothers and I all suffered from quite a bit of environmental impoverishment and poor nutrition as children, but ended up with high IQ's anyway.

I suggest that we all face it: the fact that human cranial volume has been shrinking over the last few millennia is not, I repeat *not*, a good sign, evolutionarily speaking.

In fact, it will probably turn out to have been a very *bad* sign.

September 23, 2018

Chris Langan and John von Neumann

106. Who was/is smarter, John Von Neumann or Chris Langan?

I've always admired John von Neumann and greatly respected his intelligence. But still, a couple of things need to be said here.

Obviously, answering this kind of question requires a suitable measure of intelligence. Failing to specify such a measure, and for that matter a suitable definition of "intelligence", amounts to throwing open the door to any measure or definition at all, including measures and definitions which eventually turn out to be unseemly mixtures of bias and opinion.

Secondly, while I agree that John von Neumann was a very interesting person, his life was largely determined by the fact that he was a relatively coddled child prodigy who was fast-tracked every inch of the way through it. My life has been lived much "closer to the bone", so to speak. (Yes, von Neumann was a genius, but there are many geniuses out there who didn't get all of his opportunities.)

Thirdly, in order to make an authoritative comparison between two people, one must know an appreciable amount about both of them. But while many people know a great deal about John von Neumann, relatively few know anything at all about me, and even fewer know anything about my work (a topic of great confusion among so-called "experts" in science and philosophy).

January 6, 2018

Danger zone

107. Why do some people with slightly high IQ's (120-135) think they are so great?

People with slightly or moderately above-average intelligence may fancy themselves possessed of intellectual greatness because of something very much like the Dunning-Kruger effect, which is not merely limited to people of low ability but scales upward into what is sometimes called the "IQ danger zone".

The Dunning–Kruger effect is usually understood as a cognitive bias in which people of low intellectual ability, due to their own metacognitive incapacity, imagine that they are intellectually superior. But the meaning of "low intellectual ability" is relative, which suggests that it exhibits no absolute IQ cut-off below the level at which metacognitive competence is unavoidable.

In fact, the Dunning–Kruger Effect scales up through what is sometimes called "the danger zone", approximately IQ 135–150, and sometimes higher. The danger zone syndrome is typified by those who, being experientially convinced of their own relatively high intelligence, are further encouraged by egotism, narcissism, and/or other personality disorder(s) to forget or willfully disregard their own intellectual limitations, thus displaying what amounts to metacognitive incapacity.

The danger-zone syndrome is very common among people in positions of wealth, power, and leadership, particularly those who confuse their own lack of moral inhibition with intelligence. Psychopaths and sociopaths tend to be ethically uninhibited, as it conduces to the acquisition of wealth and power at the expense of others, including those who are more capable. Foolishly equating morality to stupidity, they come to believe that ethically inhibited people are their intellectual inferiors – after all, have the morally inhibited not let morality tie their hands, thus showing themselves to be "losers" and therefore "stupid"? – and fall into a spiral of excessive self-esteem which the approval or adulation of others can only reinforce.

This is how the minds of danger-zone psychopaths and sociopaths often work, leading them to severely underestimate their betters. A great many of the world's problems can be traced to such people, who frequently manage to overtake and displace their moral and intellectual superiors from positions of responsibility and reward for which the latter are objectively much better-qualified.

Obviously, this represents a serious net loss of social and intellectual efficiency to mankind.

October 12, 2017

Economic opportunity

108. Assuming that intelligence is defined by either I.Q. or crystallized knowledge, do you know any really smart people who work dumb jobs?

I'm sorry to burst anyone's bubble, but there is no direct relationship between IQ and economic opportunity. In the supposed interests of fairness and "social justice", the natural relationship has been all but obliterated.

Consider the first necessity of employment, filling out a job application. A generic job application does not ask for information on IQ. If such information is volunteered, this is likely to be interpreted as boastful exaggeration, narcissism, excessive entitlement, exceptionalism (you're a prima donna, think you're "special", and may break the rules), and/or a lack of team spirit. None of these interpretations is likely to get you hired.

Instead, the application contains questions about job experience and educational background, neither of which necessarily has anything to do with IQ. Universities are in business for profit; they are run like companies, seek as many paying clients as they can get, and therefore routinely accept people with lukewarm IQ's, especially if they fill a slot in some quota system (in which case they will often be allowed to stay despite substandard performance). Regarding the quotas themselves, these may in fact turn the tables, advantaging members of groups with lower mean IQ's than other groups. Literally anyone can get a higher education these days if one is in a position to pay the rising price despite the diminishing returns, and sometimes, people with lower IQ's are expressly advantaged in more ways than one.

These days, most decent jobs require a college education. Academia has worked relentlessly to bring this about, as it gains money and power by monopolizing the employment market across the spectrum. Because there is a glut of college-educated applicants for high-paying jobs, there is usually no need for an employer to deviate from general policy and hire an applicant with no degree. What about the civil service? While the civil service was once mostly open to people without college educations, this is no longer the case, and quotas make a very big difference in who gets hired. Back when I was in the New York job market, "minorities" (actually, worldwide majorities) were being spotted 30 (thirty) points on the civil service exam; for example, a Black person with a score as low as 70 was hired ahead of a White person with a score of 100. Obviously, any prior positive correlation between IQ and civil service employment has been reversed.

Add to this the fact that many people, including employers, resent or feel threatened by intelligent people – especially ones who resemble men instead of pasty little geeks – and the IQ-parameterized employment function is no longer what it was once cracked up to be. If you doubt it, just look at the people running things these days. They may run a little above average, but you'd better not be expecting to find any Aristotles or Newtons among them. Intelligence has been replaced in the job market with an increasingly poor substitute, possession of a college degree, and given that education has steadily given way to indoctrination and socialization as academic priorities, it would be naive to suppose that this is not dragging down the overall efficiency of society.

In short, there are presently many highly intelligent people working very "dumb" jobs, and conversely, many less intelligent people working jobs that would once have been filled by their intellectual superiors. Those sad stories about physics PhD's flipping burgers at McDonald's are no longer so exceptional.

Sorry, folks, but this is not your grandfather's meritocracy any more.

June 25, 2017

IQ distribution map

[source map unavailable]

109.   How do you interpret this map of IQ scores?

Permission to speak frankly? Because IQ is mostly a matter of nature rather than nurture, different genetic groups – groups that evolved in different parts of the world, facing different environmental (natural and social) stressors requiring different adaptations – have different mean IQ scores.

Note that China, which is (relatively) genetically homogeneous, has a mean IQ over 105. But surprisingly, the nations whose majority inhabitants are descended from those responsible for building Western Civilization from the ground up, in whom we would expect to see the highest mean IQ's, seem to have slightly lower mean IQ's, e.g., 95 or 100. This is because

(1) Western nations are no longer genetically homogeneous, but have admitted groups with lower mean IQ's in very large numbers (often irrationally preferring those groups with the lowest mean IQ's);

(2) Western Civilization is dominated by an extremely disloyal and pathologically self-interested overclass which wants to lord it over a tractable, easily governed underclass that cannot think and cohere well enough to challenge the power structure or question the "wisdom" of its superiors therein.

In other words, the Western parasitic elite, having coopted "liberalism" and "progressivism" using the power of money, have systematically destroyed the genetic uniformity, family values, and public education systems of Western nations, "dumbing down" their populations in comparison with certain other IQ-adapted nations which do not subscribe to multiculturalism.

I know that this isn't what many people want to hear, but it's as simple as that.

January 4, 2018

In marriage

110.   How does someone with a genius-level IQ avoid making his/her spouse feel inferior? To me, intelligence has no bearing on the worth or value of a person, how can I make him/her understand this?

Find and marry an intelligent spouse, and then sincerely compliment his/her intelligence occasionally.

One need not be measurably as intelligent as one's partner. Throw a little love, creativity, and mutual respect into the mix, and intellectual disparities cannot detract from anyone's self-esteem. After all, it takes someone special to satisfy someone more intelligent, and that's not just lip service.

January 28, 2017

Race

111.   If a scientific study supports the intelligence and superiority of white man, would it be published? And why?

No study purported to show that one racial group is intellectually superior to another can be published in the present ideological climate of Academia, Inc.. The reasons are at least twofold:

(1) Academia must pursue a "big tent" admissions policy in order to maximize its tuition profit. (Regarding Whites in particular: as people of European descent are a worldwide minority relative to other "major"

racial groups, they have less money to offer in the long run than other more populous groups, and are therefore increasingly likely to find themselves holding the short end of the academic stick.)

(2) In order to stay in business at all, academia must stay on the right side of the entities which regulate it and/or ultimately provide most of its additional funding. These, of course, are global / multinational corporations and the governments with which they "partner", both of which find it advantageous to exploit modern "identity politics" as a part of their overall divide-and-conquer strategy for world domination. (We're not talking about "world democracy", by the way, but about something more akin to the EU, which has reposed all of its political power in a group of unelected bureaucrats operating on behalf of anonymous oligarchs who prefer to remain behind the curtain as a matter of personal privacy and security.)

For these reasons, and of course the avoidance of interracial strife, radical egalitarianism is a main feature of the standard ideology promoted in academia. Obviously, testing the elitist and egalitarian hypotheses would require unbiased research, and this is simply impossible at the present time.

January 19, 2017

In society

112.   How would the world react to a man who seems to combine Von Neumann's brilliance, Tesla's ingenuity and Einstein's/ Gödel's depth times ten?

That all depends on what the world, and specifically those who run the world, think they can get out of such a man.

We all like to think of ourselves as uncompromising individuals. But as a bit of honest reflection will reveal, one "sells oneself to the rich" whenever one accepts a bank loan, a position of corporate, political, or bureaucratic responsibility, or for that matter a paid job of any kind from them. A man willing to sell himself and his potential to the wealthy and powerful and to dedicate himself primarily to their interests will do fine, provided that they fairly reward him for his services and make him rich like themselves. But where egocentrism, narcissism, and deceit outweigh empathy, compassion, and loyalty in climbing the ladder of material success, this is an increasingly improbable outcome. When people sell their souls to the devil, as most people do without even realizing it, the devil has every intention of cheating them blind, and he makes no exceptions for the highly intelligent. As always, the object is to steal their patents, break contracts or promises, offshore their jobs, pass them over for well-deserved promotions in favor of relatives and sycophants, make them train cheaper replacements before laying them off, steal their pensions, tax and gouge them silly, and so on *ad nauseam*.

That's the down side of our modern pseudo-meritocracy. The up side is that if one defies the odds and manages to capitalize on one's talents without being robbed and cheated, then the world – which is in perennial bondage to the elite and suffers from the global equivalent of the Stockholm syndrome – will kiss one's rear end just for being rich! After all, one has "made the most of one's opportunities" and "made something of oneself", financially speaking (as success is usually measured, its ultimate currency is currency, period). In this event, one ends up sitting on top of the world as a "winner", as opposed to having the world write one off as a "loser" before skidding its cold, runny nose, like that of a freezing, starving orphan, across the shop window of the global economy to gaze in wonderment and envy at the next smug, sociopathic, and above all lucky and entitled social-media whiz-kid billionaire to streak across the sky ... who will, in the splendor of his riches, be compared to Einstein and Tesla whether he deserves it or not. (And he usually does not, by a very wide margin.)

On the other hand, a truly brilliant man who prefers not to spend his life chasing money had best become a hermit, hide behind the walls of an institution like a church or a university (which will claim part or all of his soul in return for its shelter), or learn to dissemble, pursuing a double-life strategy and passing himself off as relatively normal. This will help him blend in with the rest of society, whose regard for money is the only thing that protects the rich from its implacable envy and resentment. The last thing he wants is for the public to regard him as super-intelligent, as this may not only trigger hostility, but may cause people to assume that he is wealthy, and thus to double or triple the prices of even the most basic goods and services that they sell him. (Think of it as a crippling form of taxation on those perceived as wealthy, but who lack the actual wealth to retaliate legally against those who cheat them.)

Of course, such a man should also resign himself to being parasitized by the elite in any event, as this is simply what they do to everyone who can't stop them (it's a frog-and-scorpion thing. ;)

December 25, 2016

University admissions

113. Despite having an IQ of 160, I did not get into Harvard. I even submitted proof of being in Mensa. How can I cope with this and move on with my life?

The first step toward reconciliation is to realize that it is more honorable these days to be in Mensa than it is to be at Harvard. Anyone who scores above the threshold on the MENSA Test will be admitted to MENSA, no discrimination allowed. But if you're a US citizen with the bad luck to be a member of the ethnic majority (White and of European Christian ancestry), like the Founding Fathers of the United States or Harvard itself, for example, then your chances of being admitted to Harvard are far lower than they should be.

The student body of Harvard was recently found to have an American majority enrollment of a bit under 20%, far lower than one would expect on the basis of academic ability. There is simply no way to explain this except as a function of racial, national, and/or religious discrimination. Quite simply, the people who run Harvard despise people of White European ancestry, especially if there happens to be some Christianity in the mix. Evidently, this group is not sufficiently PC and "diverse" enough for them. Multiculturalism, not merit, is the primary consideration.

It's hardly an honor to be accepted by an institution which boasts of being America's most elite while discriminating viciously against the American majority. No matter what your own ethnicity may be, thank your lucky stars that you haven't been implicated in its vile Cultural Marxist social engineering program, which amounts to a criminal conspiracy to destroy the United States from within and deliver its people into slavery. Better to have clean hands even if they're not full of money.

[**Addendum** (from Comments): "I have heard Canadian Psychologist Jordan Peterson making the same point as you do in your last paragraph re social constructivism and cultural Marxism. What makes you think that this is done with the intent of bringing down the US, rather than their purported motive of compassion for marginalised groups?"

In Marxism, "the end justifies the means" is axiomatic. Marxists are allowed and in fact encouraged to lie – it's explicit in their playbook. For a Marxist/communist, literally anything is justified to bring about the Dictatorship of the Proletariat ... i.e., the dictatorship of Marxist activists and ideologues. (Yes, right-wingers lie too, but at least some of them actually feel guilty about it.)

Marxist strategists long ago announced their intention to subvert and control America by mass deception and the systematic infiltration of its power structure, including academia and the mass media. And what do we now see? Extreme leftward bias in the corporate media, monopolization of intellectual commerce and high-level employment by leftist indoctrination mills/credentials factories like Harvard, politicians openly funded and controlled by Marxist organizations and front groups, Marxist platitudes and policies coming out of their mouths and pens and legislative deliberations in great profusion, and the openly hostile presence of certain problematical "marginalized" groups which did not arise in the US, but are being imported by the millions with full governmental knowledge of their unassimilability and the danger they pose to American unity and security.

This unmistakably implies the presence of enemies within, and our "friends" the Marxists are looking very good for it ... certainly better than anyone else. It remains only to note that as always, the Marxists are secretly in bed with the wealth-and-power elite, as we see by the fact that corrupt corporate fascists like George Soros are funding domestic socialist groups, paying rabble-rousers and demonstrators to riot, and generally fueling unrest with no resistance or explicit disapproval by the government. The ultimate goal has become obvious: a 2-tier neofeudal society with corporate fascism at the top as always, and communism for all the "little people" down at the bottom (that way, people won't ask why the rich have so much and they so little; they will concentrate on trying to stay alive while jealously watching each other to make sure that their rich masters have no annoying competition from lowly members of the proletariat).

Every time the Marxists take over and rule a nation, it's only a matter of time before its citizens are disarmed, relieved of their freedom, and standing in bread lines, where they talk in very low voices lest the wrong word send them to the gulag, reeducation camp, or killing field.

Meanwhile, the party elite – and of course, those by whom they are financially leveraged – fatten on the blood of the people, gorging until their wealth, power, and privilege exceed all bounds. This is the way it went in Russia, China, Romania, Yugoslavia, and Cambodia ... and how it's going right here, right now, in the Americas. It's a massive, murderous, phenomenally abusive pseudo-utopian scam run by con artists with big ambitions and very little in the way of humanity, and it's strictly for dummies.

If that's really what you want, it can only be because you think you'll be part of the inner circle, the Politburo, the Supreme Soviet. But the problem is, so do you all ... and at best, only a handful of you will make it. So the question is, how much of your soul will you sell to make the cut? ;)]

October 20, 2017

Verbal IQ

114.   What is this verbal IQ thing? I've never heard of it before.

Intelligence manifests in many ways. These have been reduced to a set of "intelligence factors" which can to some extent be separately tested. In addition, there is a general intelligence (meta)factor called "g" which shows up in composite scores based on multiple tests, and which in principle is expressed across all IQ factors and subtests.

Due to the cognitive universality of g, an IQ test can in principle test for just one factor (or irreducible complex of factors) in a given factorization of intelligence and still be reasonably accurate in providing an "estimate" of IQ. However, due to impairment, disability, or a developmental deficit, problems may occur which can lead to asymmetry among the factors (as when one or more factors are simultaneously tested at levels significantly below most of the others for a given test subject). Thus, while an IQ test including only a single factor is not always as accurate or reliable as a multi-factor test, it can provide a fairly good estimate of overall cognitive ability even where problems exist with regard to other factors.

An all-verbal IQ test typically measures such abilities as vocabulary, language comprehension, conceptual abstraction and discernment, and general knowledge or "crystallized intelligence". At one time, such tests were fairly common.

That being said, there is no getting away from language in any intelligence test whatsoever, as some form of language must be employed to communicate the tasks and deliver the responses.

February 16, 2018

Wealth

115. Are smartest people the richest too? Is there any correlation between intelligence and being rich?

"Wealth = power," yes. "Wealth = intelligence," never. The wealth = intelligence equation is absurd on its face.

One can be born rich, but due to upper class inbreeding and sheer mental laziness, quite slow. On the other hand, if one is born poor, one very probably lacks the wealth and connections that it certainly takes to accumulate large amounts of capital by modern standards. Due to the structure of the economic system, capital attracts capital, and where large concentrations of capital accumulate, connections with other rich people accumulate as well. Hence the old aphorism "It takes money to make money." Quite simply, when you're rich, other rich people, and people aspiring to be rich, want to be your friends. But if you're poor, good luck getting past security.

The matter is complicated by several other factors. Competitive advantages like ego, ambition, deceit, and a psychopathic willingness to manipulate others arguably outweigh intellectual brilliance on the scales of material success, and even where intellectual superiority exists, its competitive advantages may be neutralized by financially irrelevant traits like morality and compassion. And of course, if one has been raised to believe that rich people are inordinately selfish and cannot be trusted, one will tend to avoid them, which in most cases means avoiding their money as well.

Lastly, brilliant people often have things on their minds which they rightly consider to be more important than chasing money, especially given that the competition for money is so fierce that accumulating it from scratch tends to demand all of one's time and mental resources, pushing more important and/or socially responsible priorities aside.

December 21, 2016

116.   Is there something wrong with the idea that if I'm not smart enough to change the world, I can be rich enough to hire smart people to the change world?

Yes, there is something very wrong with the premise that one who is not smart enough to change the world for the better can make up for it by getting rich enough to hire smart people to change the world for the better. The problem is that if one is not smart enough to know how to change the world for the better – and this takes more intelligence than one might think – then one is not necessarily smart enough to conclusively identify people who are smart enough to know how to change the world for the better, and will therefore be in no position to hire them (unless one gets lucky).

The intellectual requirements for being rich are far less stringent than those for knowing how to change the world for the better. Yet the rich, always craving praise and publicity, want to justify their materialism after the fact, and to expiate their (often spectacular) transgressions on the way to success by providing smarter and more dedicated people with financial resources to do what the rich lack the brainpower to do themselves. This sometimes yields limited success, but it cannot as a rule be done efficiently; a rich nincompoop can too easily make a bad situation worse by planting himself and his employees in the middle of it when it requires better minds, even displacing the very people who could otherwise have dealt with it in the right way.

Nevertheless, this get-rich-and-throw-money-at-it routine is the rule rather than the exception. Name a high-profile problem, and it's only a matter of time before some wealthy dunce decides to become a big star by hurling himself and his money at it, usually by scouring academia for highly credentialed academics who can point out other academics whom he can hire to make him the Savior of Mankind and get his mug on the cover of Time Magazine despite the fact that his own head contains nothing but rocks and dollar signs.

Unfortunately, it's not usually that simple. Truly profound solutions for extremely hard problems do not usually come about as a function of wishful thinking and financially stimulated academic nepotism. We know this because there are too many big, important problems that academics have chronically failed to solve no matter how much time and money they were given to do it.

However, a note of caution is appropriate. If the only alternative to misguided philanthropy and private enterprise is handing everything over to the government, then misguided philanthropy and private enterprise it will have to be. For you see, in this inverse meritocracy we inhabit, it's as Ronald Reagan used to say: "The nine most terrifying words in the English language are: "I'm from the government, and I'm here to help." Help of the kind we're accustomed to getting from the government is often considerably worse than no help at all.

December 12, 2017

117. Is Chris Langan correct that we "have no business equating wealth with intelligence"? Some of my few Republican colleagues seem to do just that, and more.

Of course I'm right.

Granted, IQ and income are somewhat positively correlated; people with higher IQ's tend to make more money, at least below a certain limit. However, the strength of the correlation does not support the inference of a definite causal relationship. On the other hand, the relationship between IQ and wealth is all over the place, suggesting that there is no such thing as a social-Darwinistic wealth-based meritocracy. There's a touch of meritocracy in the distribution of income – it peters out very quickly as we go higher on the IQ scale – but not in the ownership of large mansions and fat investment portfolios. It turns out that the hereditary rich, lucky investors, etc., have nothing very special going on upstairs.

Unfortunately, this is a problem. Just as the power to affect the course of society is amplified by wealth, the ill effects of the relative moral and intellectual deficiencies of the rich are *also* amplified by wealth. In short, the rich are not in general sufficiently intelligent to properly use their wealth and influence to guide us toward a better world, especially in the presence of as many diversions and distractions as now assail us, and their wealth and power only amplify their mistakes. The common "meritocracy assumption" – that wealth correlates with intelligence and responsibility throughout the IQ scale – turns out to be so much hot air, and due to the inevitable "wealth = power" equation, systemic injustices of the real economy translate directly into socioeconomic degeneration.

In other words, it is simply not true that as the power of the wealthy to determine the evolution of society increases as a function of net worth, they are proportionally capable of manifesting the integrity and intelligence to provide society with optimum guidance and financial impetus. The meritocracy assumption is just a variant of the illusory "just world hypothesis" and the associated conception of "justice" according to which reward is always proportional to merit. We do not live in a just world, and the rich are not on top of society because God put them there.

Of course, there supposedly exists a patch for this situation. It's called "Academia, Inc.", from which the uber-wealthy and powerful are supposedly able to hire experts who know how to make judgments and solve problems that the rich lack the brainpower to handle on their own. But unfortunately, academia – in its own special bureaucratic way – is every bit as degenerate as the investment class; in effect, it is led around by its nose at the merest scent of money, whoring out like a drug-addicted hooker at any hint of the long green. (I'm terribly sorry if this offends anyone, but it is what it is.)

Add to this the fact that academia and its minions systematically exclude any outsider who tries to participate meaningfully in intellectual commerce – that is, anyone lacking not only wealth, but credentials and connections – and the problem becomes obvious to anyone with half a brain (which naturally excludes fat cats and acadummies. ;)

December 28, 2017

L

LANGAN, CHRIS

Intelligence

118. Are there really self-educated geniuses from the streets like in Good Will Hunting?

Of course there are. Back in the late 1990's, possibly inspired by the success of "Good Will Hunting", reporters began looking around for someone like the character. It seems that they found me, after which I appeared on every major television network in North America and many others abroad.

I've never met anyone involved with the movie, and I'm sure that none of the cast or producers had ever heard of me. So what made people think that I was something approaching a real-world template for the movie character? Well, I had a rough home life growing up. I barely have a high school diploma – they didn't even want to give me one of those – but I can make almost any professional academic look like a dunce at will. I've worked as a cowboy, construction worker, firefighter, and fisherman, and I was perhaps the best-known bar bouncer in the Greater New York area for 25 years. I was the first person ever to solve the venerable chicken-or-egg problem (my solution is the one for which somebody else is credited anew every two or three years). I'm even the author of the CTMU, the one and only viable theory of mathematical metaphysics.

Despite all that, I'm sure that most people have no idea who I am. I don't really care, as I've always been a private person (the press always contacted me, never vice versa). But if I had to guess at the reasons, there are at least three that I might consider. One is Academia, which runs a closed shop and monopolizes scientific communication and intellectual commerce to the complete exclusion of outsiders. Another is that IQ has been deconstructed and democratized until everyone and his dog thinks of himself or herself as a genius. (Everyone deserves to be respected for his or her special intellectual attributes, but I suspect that many people have gone a little overboard in the self-esteem department these days.) Yet another is that I'm a White male who dared to use the forbidden G-word (God) when questioned about what I believed, and was mercilessly disparaged and defamed by every half-baked atheistic troll on the planet in revenge for my theological opinions.

But enough. If you want to read more, you can try this link:

https://superscholar.org/interviews/christopher-michael-langan/

July 6, 2017

119. Is Christopher Langan the smartest person in the world?

I agree with the idea, more or less stated in another comment, that being smart and having a high IQ are not necessarily equivalent properties. But this makes judging intelligence all the more difficult. To be judged extraordinarily intelligent, one must communicate extraordinary thoughts to those doing the judging. But this raises a vexing issue: as any really intelligent person knows, communication is always a two-way street. This is not only because communication consists of at least two people exchanging information, but because each must understand what the other is saying. Unfortunately, extraordinary thoughts are often extraordinarily hard for most people to understand.

As relatively few people properly understand the CTMU, it is occasionally subject to erroneous opinionation. For example, it is not self-contradictory as claimed in this Q&A, but uniquely consistent ... provably so, in fact. And at this point, perhaps the main reason – aside from bias and obstinacy – that its critics don't better understand it is that the modern system of intellectual communication and commerce dominated by Academia, Inc. has been completely walled off from those who lack the academic stamp of approval (to which, if the truth be told, any reasonable concept of intellectual excellence is increasingly irrelevant). It's a circular enterprise, a corrupt intellectual trade union that would make the Mafia blush. I can't even post a paper to arXiv – one needs an institutional affiliation for that! (So much for the alleged neutrality and infallibility of "peer review".)

Just to dispel any remaining confusion, the CTMU is absolutely serious Furthermore, it is incontrovertible. What do I mean by that? I mean that if anyone were to gather the "best" philosophers, theologians, mathematicians, and physicists from the "best" universities in the world, they couldn't put a dent in it even if those criticizing it here were helping them. They could, and would, be squashed like bugs, as publicly as one might like. If no one else were able or disposed to perform this service, I could easily handle it myself. The most with which they could get away would be an admission that the theory is unclear to them, or that they don't find it "mathematical enough". But in fact, the CTMU is a theory of metaphysics that is based *entirely* on mathematics, albeit of kinds that are not taught to most students in these fields.

Although some have maintained that the CTMU is "information-free" despite the mathematics that it obviously contains, the real truth is that they are personally incapable of registering the level of information that the CTMU conveys. For this, I can take no more than partial responsibility.

December 25, 2016

120.   Does Chris Langan really have an IQ of 200?

Perhaps. This is a psychometric extrapolation, i.e., an estimate. In principle, my IQ could be lower. On the other hand, it could be higher. (With all due respect to "the competition", I'm certainly not worried about getting shown up by anyone claiming higher intelligence, which doesn't necessarily equate to IQ anyway.)

Let's just say that there are several people for whom even higher numbers have been estimated, at least with regard to ratio as opposed to deviation IQ. So if one's idea is that actually racking up such high scores is impossible, one may as well start at the top and work one's way down.

[**Note**: This may well be a troll question, as implied by the fact that one of the two parties who requested this answer of me recently announced that he'd be trolling me. Yesterday, on February 24, 2018, in response to my answer to the question "What is Chris Langan up to these days?", in which I reported that I was being stalked by a couple of trolls, he commented as follows: "You just earned yourself another one. Have a nice day!" It isn't very often that a troll openly announces his evil intent, but when he does, his target can usually expect the trolling to begin immediately, and this A2A would seem to fit the mold. Just as suspiciously, another answer – pejorative as usual – has just been posted by one of the very stalkers to whom I'd referred. If this is about trolling, then what a shame that Quora is being used to chisel away at the credentials of notable participants. Not that it would be terribly surprising given the harassment to which I've been recurrently subjected here of late by the trolls in question.]

February 26, 2018

121. Why do so many people believe Chris Langan is super-intelligent when it is obvious to any actually intelligent person that he is putting up a facade?

I hate to disappoint any Quora trolls who may be on the lurk, but I don't rely on facades. I simply have no need of them. I can squash the vast majority of my intellectual opponents like insects, and the "tall tales" of my intelligence have been born out several times over on standard tests, experimental tests, and the body of work that carries my name.

On the other hand, the person who posted this question is evidently *very much into* facades. First, we have the fact that no name has been given; the poster is anonymous (the facade is so weak that one can't even put a name to it). Secondly, there's the pretense that whereas I (Chris Langan) am merely feigning intelligence, the poster of this question is an "*actually* intelligent person" who is peering scornfully down at me from the heights of Olympus.

Now, anyone who buys *that* kind of facade is *really* feigning intelligence! But not very convincingly, I'm afraid.

August 7, 2018

Quora

122.   Why have we seen so little of Chris Langan?

I don't think it's quite fair to say that I've been "seen so little". I've actually posted quite a few answers here, mostly of a kind that no other participant could have duplicated.

It is possible that there would be more answers from me if:

(1) a number of my contributions hadn't been eliminated to placate various trolls from whom I'd tried to defend myself and my work;

(2) the page hadn't spontaneously reloaded during my attempt to correctively comment on an answer previously provided by one of Quora's most popular science contributors, at which point comments were suddenly disabled and my corrections vanished (I got the impression that someone at Quora was able to read what I was writing in real time, and had opted to protect the answer by resetting the page to disable comments and destroy what I'd written in response).

In addition, I've notice that my comments are typically viewed far less than those of certain prolific contributors here, suggesting to me that Quora may employ a rating system or viewing policy that somehow favors high-volume contributors at the expense of lower-volume ones irrespective of quality, and/or that the readership of Quora is strongly biased toward contributors with certain viewpoints that I find insupportable.

If at some point I have reason to change my mind regarding these concerns, I may contribute more often. Quora is basically a good idea; it's just the execution that worries me.

Thanks for your interest.

June 21, 2017

Typical day

123.   What does Chris Langan's typical day look like?

Thanks for asking, but I'm afraid this may be a little boring. I live on a ranch in an isolated rural location, so there's very little in the way of nightlife and commercial entertainment. While it's very pretty and private, the virtual absence of a local service economy means that we're almost entirely on our own – for most of what needs to be done, there's no nearby tradesman able to do it competently and affordably. Self-sufficiency is an indispensable virtue.

On a typical day, I wake up and make coffee for me and my wife. We may talk for a while about what needs to be done. I sit down at my desk and work on intellectual matters, transcribing the answers to any questions that had been on my mind before I retired (I usually wake up with the answers). I check my email and catch up on any accumulated business that may have hit my inbox – I run a nonprofit foundation, and I'm sometimes included in email distributions for physicists, mathematicians, and cognitive scientists with whose technical problems I sometimes try to help.

After a while, I exit the house – a 1500 ft^2 farmhouse built at the end of the 19th century, which I've largely rebuilt over the last 12 years or so – and tend to any urgent ranch business that may have emerged during the night, doing a few chores. (There are almost no professional ranch hands anymore; even in agricultural areas such as this one, everyone wants to be a wealthy big shot like the gasbags and stuffed shirts on TV, or why work at all?) I return to the house, browse a couple of news sites to get some headlines – we have no live television connection here, just a television connected to a computer and a DVD player – and see to more business or do some more thinking and writing.

As midday approaches, my wife describes to me what she's contemplating for lunch; I tell her how good it sounds, or request a slight modification. We eat lunch. I return to my desk and do a bit more work ... how much depends on the lunch (too many carbs, and I might feel the urge to take a brief nap). I exit the house for another round of chores – feeding the animals, fortunately not an everyday necessity, consists of moving up to 20,000 pounds of hay into various pastures using either of two old but powerful JD diesel tractors. I come back inside and do some more thinking and writing. Dinner involves a slightly more elaborate repetition of the lunch routine. While the sun is still up, I go out and button everything down that needs to be secured before nightfall. I return to my desk and write until it's time to go to sleep. I might watch a movie with my wife. Reload and repeat.

Interspersed among regular activities are limited breaks consisting of recreational pastimes like reading, writing music, or pumping a little iron. Telephone usage is relatively infrequent; there's no real cell phone service in this remote location. When necessary, I make a trip to town (the two nearest towns are 8 and 10 miles away, but they lack real grocery stores, and the next-nearest towns are nearly 40 miles distant). If something requires me to catch a plane, I must leave 4-5 hours in advance because the nearest large airport is 120 miles away, and parking is often in limited supply. A recent unexpected trip to NYC for a television interview, for example, consumed two full days with almost no down time. It's hard to get away for much longer than that due to the nature of the operation.

Of course, there's plenty of *ad hoc* variation. Ranches typically have many mouths to feed, and sometimes emergencies arise. The most recent emergency, for example, was an amorous 2000 pound black Angus outside the fence ... one of my bulls, who had broken through the fence in order to court lonely cows across the road. Other kinds of emergency: an animal falls ill or gives birth; a stallion breaches the mares' pasture "without permission"; a lightning storm passes through and sends a limb or an entire tree where it shouldn't have gone, and so on. (It might even come to my attention that some logic-challenged troll has launched a polemical online attack on me or the CTMU, in which case I may attempt a little damage control ... or maybe not.)

This is all very flexible and approximate, but I'm sure you get the picture.

May 8, 2017

LOGIC

Absolute Truth

124.   Do Christians like the CTMU, the proof of God?

That all depends on whether or not they're real Christians as opposed to fake "I believe everything my duly ordained priest / pastor says and nothing else" Christians.

People who believe in Christian Scripture *must* believe in the CTMU, as scripture must be interpreted in logic in order to be apprehended, and the CTMU is merely logic formulated on the required level of discourse.

On the other hand, fake Christians cannot apprehend scripture except by filtering it through layers of doctrine authored by fallible human beings pretending to have divined its proper interpretation. This means that they cannot directly apprehend scripture at all, hence cannot meet the most fundamental requirement of true Christianity.

There's a big difference between real and fake Christians. Christ himself would have told you to choose logic over doctrine, as it is immediate to God. In fact, God and Christ are scripturally identified with logic in the form of "Logos" or Absolute Truth [John 1:1].

(We'll keep it short due to the troll problem here at Quora – questions and answers have a strange way of simply disappearing, and I have only so much time to spend, and potentially to waste, on such a volatile medium.)

July 12, 2018

125.   What do you consider the true religion and why?

If one wants a belief system based on Absolute Truth, then one needs to have identified Absolute Truth ... or, as it is called in Christianity, Logos. It has been scripturally approximated in Christianity itself, and is even personified by Christ. However, its mathematical structure is not identified in any known body of scripture.

There is just one well-defined comprehensive truth-structure, or knowledge-system, based on Absolute Truth. It has not been promoted as a religion, but merely described as a "metareligion" in which other religions

118

are subject to interpretation. Technically, it would be classified as a metaphysical formulation of logic. It has been here for decades, but has never been embraced or even acknowledged by spokesmen for major organized religions (or minor disorganized ones, for that matter). Such people usually say what they must to ensure maximum popular and financial support for themselves and (secondarily) their own creeds; deny it though they might, logic and truth are strictly side-issues for them.

This truth-structure is called the CTMU, and it's been out there for decades. There is not a philosopher, theologian, mathematician, or scientist on Earth who is remotely knowledgeable or intelligent enough to gainsay a single word of it. (This is not to disparage anyone's intellectual ability; it's a function of how the system is structured. As its author, I know this with certainty. I'm relatively well-known, yet I have never seen a valid, meaningful, content-oriented critique of it from anyone with any weight in the field. Given that I'm better-known than most of those who would be doing the critiquing, the reason can only be that no real authority has the knowledge or confidence to take issue with it.)

Those who go on spiritual quests for the ultimate spiritual system should beware, as this is a very noisy field; there is a great deal of unwarranted competition for peoples' attention. The loudest and most insistent voices usually belong to the most venal and ambitious people. I would sincerely advise readers against embracing any other system to the exclusion of the CTMU, as there would be a spiritual cost associated with doing so.

I hope everyone has a great day.

October 8, 2017

Branch of philosophy

126. Why is logic a branch of philosophy?

Logic consists of the rules for attributing properties to objects (predicate logic), and for determining whether the resulting attributions are true or false (propositional or sentential logic). Thus, it is integral to ontology, which concerns attributions of existence, and epistemology, which concerns the ability to know attributions as true or false.

Ontology and epistemology are coinciding aspects of metaphysics, which is central to philosophy insofar as it spans all that exists, or – placing the emphasis on epistemology rather than ontology – of all that can be known.

Hence, logic has everything to do with philosophy on the deepest possible level, and vice versa.

July 28, 2018

Human Cognitive-Perceptual Syntax

127. Can something be conceived without any axiom?

Yes, to the extent that it instantiates the (self-instantiating) *a priori* HCPS (*Human Cognitive-Perceptual Syntax*). The HCPS, which can be understood as the accepting syntax of any human observer (or a generic observer defined thereon), is necessary and therefore universal because nothing can be conceived or perceived without it.

Note that it would be correct to substitute *logic* for "the HCPS" in the above paragraph. However, this would require that *logic* be defined to accommodate the CTMU, a truly universal and therefore metaphysical formulation of logic which applies not just to generic attributions, but to the entirety of logic and all that goes with it.

In contrast, theoretically induced axioms usually refer to hypothetical *a posteriori* content without which they cannot be fully instantiated, and their universality is not given for any universe not defined on them by fiat.

May 30, 2018

Intelligibility of reality

128. What if the CTMU were correct?

This question is equivalent to "What if *logic* were correct on the metaphysical (metalogical, metamathematical) level of reality and all levels beneath?"

The answer is very simple: Logic / the CTMU must be correct on all levels of reality, for if it were not, then reality would be unintelligible, in which case there would be no science, philosophy, mathematics, or reality as we know it.

So really, all that one need do is decide how much one likes science, philosophy, mathematics, and reality itself, and then answer accordingly.

; -)

March 29, 2018

Interpretation of scripture and observations

129.   Which tells the truth, Bible or science?

In a way, this is a meaningless question. Truth is a logical property; its structure can be considered that of logic in its entirety. Science and religion are true only insofar as they can be interpreted in logic, or shown to be logically consistent and thus to "model logic", and the jury remains out until this requirement is satisfied.

Science can be interpreted in logic with respect to direct replicable observation and the immediate logical entailments thereof; beyond that, it relies on empirical induction and does not support claims of truth or proof. Religion is even more problematic, especially when based on revelatory scripture; miracles are by definition non-replicable in any reliable sense, and must therefore be taken on faith by those who do not witness them directly.

Although the Bible is based on a powerful set of universal (and therefore unfalsifiable) truths, some of which are shared or "replicated" by other religions, its revelatory and universal contents make it impossible to completely verify using standard scientific methodology. However, **this does not rule out substantial verification by means of logic**, which in any event has always been the sole means of verification beyond the perceptual realm. Using a sufficiently advanced form of logic, it can be shown that Christianity is largely based on verifiable (true, logically self-consistent) principles.

It thus turns out that both science and the Bible are verifiable with respect to direct objective perception of the external world and all logical necessities thereof. Because they can both be largely interpreted in the same advanced logical system or "truth structure", they can in fact be shown to correspond with each other in certain key respects. It is thus meaningless to call either one of them "more true" than the other; they are simply concomitant aspects of reality.

While this may be reassuring, a word of caution is in order: neither science nor religion is immune to error and confusion. It is thus a very good thing that through their mutual dependency on logic, each is a potential source of improvement for the other.

February 10, 2017

Logic vs physical naturalism

130. What would require you to give up your naturalistic worldview in order to embrace the truth of Christopher Langan's Cognitive-Theoretic Model of the Universe?

I'll answer this one, if I may: as I've previously explained elsewhere on this site, **logic** is what requires the rejection of (naive physical) naturalism. The CTMU is logic in the sense that it is a globally distributed ingredient of reality which contains no assumptions or nontautological axioms, and it precludes naive naturalism due to its referential incapacity for self-explanation.

As the CTMU has been out there for thirty years or so, we can no longer say that the technical relationship between this universe and global reality is "in its infancy" (as another answer claims). In fact, it is quite evolved and robust. What remains in its infancy is the openness of academia and its journals to material emanating from anyone but certified, dues-paying academics, who have a mile-wide conflict of interest when it comes to serving truth over their own collective interests, and of course, over the interests of the shady, similarly conflicted proprietors of their glorified trade union / corporate monopoly.

Once that conflict of interest is resolved, and the honor and chastity of truth have been rightfully restored, the world can more easily take account of existing developments in the field of mathematical metaphysics.

February 13, 2018

Nature of tautology

131. Why do people assume that the CTMU contains assumptions when, in fact, it doesn't?

People erroneously assume that the CTMU contains assumptions because assumption is their intellectual default condition. They fall back on assumption because they are intellectually incapable of discerning the necessities on which human knowledge is actually based.

Knowledge entails certainty by definition, and certainty entails logic. Logic is based not on assumption, but on tautology (tautological forms and inferences). Without fully understanding the structural and dynamical properties and manifestations of tautology, they simply assume that nothing of scientific interest can ever be logically deduced from well-verified initial data.

This assumption is very common but ultimately mistaken. The irony is that because so many people stumble into it – including many highly trained people who are supposed to know better – those who rightly question it are the ones usually accused of "making assumptions".

Eventually, one learns to see this situation as rather comical, like a passel of clowns frantically unicycling around the center ring, bumping into each other and toppling over and generally creating mayhem under the Big Top while cacophonously squeezing the air out of their red rubber noses. ;)

April 26, 2018

Predicate logic

132. Is predicate logic dualistic as stated in the latest CTMU paper published in the academic, philosophical journal Cosmos and History?

That's what it says in the papers, right?

Predicate logic is dualistic because it considers attributes separately from the objects or arguments to which they are attached by (universal or existential) quantification.

Equivalently, predicate logic is a formal system which includes a formal language (including its formal grammar) and a deductive apparatus consisting of axioms and rules of inference. The external universe is excluded from the system, isolating the language from the rest of reality.

July 11, 2018

Properties of logic

133. Is logic learned? Is it absolute or relative? Is it influenced at all by society?

As the term is ordinarily used, logic is a fundamental requirement of human experience that is universal and unvarying. This must be the case insofar as it governs the coupling of objects and attributes (predicate logic), permits the discernment of logical complements (propositional logic), and controls implication and entailment (determines how one thing follows from another).

Logic is innate and *a priori* to the extent that its failure on the level of sensory perception and basic reasoning would preclude the individual and consensual identification of physical reality and its ingredients, preventing discernment of objects, relations, and events. This is confirmed by the fact that regardless of our logical training, we all perceive the same physical world and can agree on what it contains. The fact that we all inhabit the same world, consisting of the same physical objects, relationships, events, and processes, attests to the unconditional invariance and universality of logic.

The perfect distribution of logic over physical reality and valid cognition is a hard requirement of empirical science, which depends on the replicability of observation and the unbroken possibility of valid inference. Conversely, the existence of empirical science implies that given any apparent violation of logic, we can always resolve the paradox and restore consistency.

While pathological deviations from logic are not precluded, we are assured that when such deviations collide with reality, reality and logic will ultimately prevail.

April 17, 2018

Propositional logic

134. Why are propositional and predicate logic important in
the CTMU?

For the same reason that they are important in science and philosophy in
general: predicate logic is basic to attribution, while propositional logic is
required for classifying attributions as true or false. (Technically, propositional logic is properly included in predicate logic; after all, truth values
are attributes.) One cannot have a meaningful theory without them.

However, there are differences between the CTMU and standard theories
with regard to where logic resides, the particular form it takes, and how
it is applied.

June 25, 2018

Self-justifying nature of tautology

135. The CTMU says tautologies are self-justifying. How can this
be true?

A statement can be proven true or false – in fact, it can be *identified* – only
by using 2-valued propositional logic. Therefore, 2-valued propositional
logic is verified by the identifiability or provability of anything at all.

A specific propositional tautology amounts to an axiom of 2-valued logic;
thus, it is implicated in its own identification. As it can be identified
only if it is true, we know that it *must* be true by the mere fact that we
can identify it.

The CTMU develops this idea in order to elevate the field of mathematical logic to the metaphysical level of discourse, the better to answer
profound questions that empirical scientists insist on asking, but lack
the tools to answer.

And now a brief word regarding the anti-CTMU trolls which proliferate like a toxic fungus here at Quora. There is no one on Quora who
is remotely smart enough, or good enough at math, logic, philosophy,
physics, chemistry, biology, or anything else, to get over on the CTMU.
In fact, the mere effort to get over on the CTMU, and for that matter on

me, is incontrovertible, rock-hard proof that the person trying to do it is a logical ignoramus, a nincompoop, and a buffoon. The nastier he or she is about it, the more he or she is attempting to mislead the readership of Quora, and the more he or she deserves censure as an absolute gibbering idiot.

Let's be clear about this. There are people on Quora who claim to have advanced degrees in this or that from big-name universities; some are even lauded as "Quora Top Writers", whatever that's supposed to mean. So far, so good. But after tooting their own horns like the steam-powered pufferbellies of yore, some of them have revealed themselves as mean-spirited imbeciles by flying into protracted fits of projectile diarrhea of the mouth, calling the theory "bullshit", "horse shit", "crap", and "nonsense". Alleged upvotes notwithstanding, the readers of Quora would be vastly better off without a single one of them.

I'm tired of having to make a hobby out of digging everyone else out from under the piles of manure spewed by these people. It would be wonderful if they could simply run off and find another topic about which to blow smoke up everyone else's rectum while knowing not a damned thing about it.

Thanks for your attention.

June 29, 2018

Structure of truth

136. Are all truths logical?

Yes, as logic can be described as the "definition" or "structure" of truth.

However, the truth predicate takes attributions as its arguments, and the *signature* or "alphabet" of the language in which a given truth is expressed may contain symbols representing both *logical* and *nonlogical* elements, where by "logical elements" we mean the symbols and associated concepts of mathematical logic, and by "nonlogical elements" we mean (e.g.) symbols representing concepts like *point, line,* and *angle* in the signature of the language of geometry. So the truth need not be exclusively logical or even logically determined; it may involve nonlogical elements and be freely determined by nonlogical considerations.

That being understood, every nonlogical language must conform to logic in order to be intelligible – it must fit into appropriate logical expressions as instances thereof – and in this sense, logic and truth are inseparable.

October 11, 2017

137.   Could God prove his existence?

Of course He could. He would simply show that His structure is that of truth and existence themselves.

It would take just two questions.

(1) What is the structure of truth and existence?

(2) What properties do you share with this structure ... i.e., how are you identified with it?

If the shared properties include those on which the "God" concept is conventionally defined, then God would have proven that He exists in the form of truth or Logos, just as stated in the New Testament. Basically, Truth is queried about itself, and divinity is recognized in its logical structure.

(I've already been through this in considerable detail, starting three or four decades ago. The relevant structure is called the CTMU, acronymic for *Cognitive Theoretic Model of the Universe*.)

June 19, 2017

Tool for studying reality

138.   Which field of science studies reality as a whole?

Technically, the answer would be "metaphysics", considered as an explanatory generalization of physics and other scientific disciplines. However, most people would argue that metaphysics is not a science, but merely an unkempt collection of abstruse philosophical ideas.

What about modern sciences? There are two general kinds of "science", *mathematical* and *empirical*. The empirical sciences are constrained by the Scientific Method and thereby limited to observation, logical deduction from observation, and empirical induction, which are inadequate for the study of reality as a whole. This suggests that the study of reality falls within the range of the mathematical sciences.

However, most mathematical theories are formulated with respect to abstract universes defined on sets of axioms which do not fully characterize empirical reality, let alone reality as a whole. They apply only to those parts of empirical reality which happen to obey their respective axioms. There is only one branch of mathematics which covers every aspect of reality without exception, including the empirical aspect: logic. This is because the truth predicate of two-valued logic can be used to denote inclusion in reality at large.

So the answer is logic, along with any other branch of mathematics, or bundle of branches, whose axioms separately or collectively cover every part of reality. A global reality theorist therefore needs, above all, to be a mathematical logician. He or she can then fit other, narrower branches of science into mathematical logic as auxiliary theories. (For example, physics is just a bundle of mathematical theories in which certain terms are observationally defined, and every mathematical theory can on some level be interpreted in a sufficiently advanced form of logic.)

Again, what I've just described is a framework for what "metaphysics" was originally supposed to be. Unfortunately, modern philosophy, which lays claim to metaphysics, has become too disconnected, disorganized, and equivocal to exhibit the coherence expected of a science. In short, too many people recognized as "philosophers" and "metaphysicians" have too long operated in too unscientific a way for their versions of "metaphysics" to qualify as scientific explanations of reality.

So for the time being, mathematical logic it is. This may not be what most people want to hear – they want something easier, or perhaps "sexier" – but it's the only discipline with an unlimited capacity for both ontological generality and scientific specificity, and thus able to accommodate all of reality without prejudice or preconception.

February 12, 2017

MASS MEDIA

Indoctrination

139. Why are people with a low IQ getting more news coverage than Chris Langan and his ideas?

This is the case because the mass media and its mass audience contain many more people of ordinary intelligence than people of extraordinary intelligence, and there is money to be made by telling people just what they can understand and want to hear.

As it happens, many people don't want to hear that there is someone more knowledgeable than they on the nature of reality, that the academic degrees and doctrines they bought so dearly aren't really a substitute for intelligence and hard-earned knowledge, that there is a God independent of their preferred body of religious or antireligious doctrine Who may discard them if they insult, disobey, or actively oppose Him, et cetera. They want to hear the exact opposite, and the establishment is only too happy to sell them what they desire.

People of normal intelligence are far more common and easier to indoctrinate than those of extraordinary intelligence. The world is run by a small but powerful minority which tells the majority what to believe and thus what it eventually wants to hear; it indoctrinates the majority to adopt and prefer irrational beliefs that violate majority interests but conduce to its own. Being a nonmember of the controlling minority, I am in no position to take advantage of the mass media or the machinery of public indoctrination in order to promote work which deviates from standard doctrine.

The highest and deepest kinds of truth have no monetary value in a materialistic society, and may even be suppressed by the controlling minority as opposing its interests. Under these circumstances, the mass media naturally prefer more orthodox, widely palatable, and therefore lucrative content.

January 13, 2018

MATHEMATICS

On conceptual abstractions

140. Is it possible to mathematically represent conceptual abstraction of Christopher Langan's Cognitive-Theoretic Model of the Universe? If so what is the proof?

Yes. In fact, it is possible to mathematically represent *any* coherent conceptual abstraction. All one needs to do is define one or more symbols to represent it and/or its components, and then specify a mathematical structure to which the symbols conform, usually something "algebraic". A language is an algebraic structure, and the CTMU is the start symbol of the grammar through which its detailed structure emerges. Now here's the cherry on the sundae: because the language in question is supertautological, its grammar is self-verifying, thus obviating the need for additional proof ... which, however, is by no means precluded. (See how easy that was?)

February 5, 2018

Illogical exclusion

141. What is the most illogical thing in mathematics?

The most illogical thing in mathematics is the exclusion of the mathematician from mathematical structures and reasoning, technically rendering mathematicians powerless to reliably understand or connect with the content of their field. This systematic exclusion has been prolonged by the exclusion from mathematical journals of anything resembling a valid correction.

April 14, 2018

On infinitesimals

142. Could we "invent" a number h = 1/0 similarly to the way we "invented" i = sqrt (-1)? What would be the effect on modern math if we did so?

This number already exists in the form of "infinity". However, there is a cheat involved: "0" becomes the infinitesimal "1/infinity", which is "of measure 0" in the real unit interval. That is, 0 is interpreted as a "measure" rather than a quantity, and a nonzero "infinitesimal" *quantity* is invented which coincides with *measure* 0. This can be expressed as follows: "An infinitesimal is a nonzero number that is less than any *finite* quantity, and is therefore quantitatively negligible, i.e., has sub-finite *measure* 0."

It's quite a trick; *quantity* has been disjoined from *measure* using the term *infinitesimal* and then crudely plastered back together with measure using the phrase "measure 0". An infinitesimal is a *nonzero* quantity representing *zero* progress along a line segment. The cost is that infinity "breaks" finite algebra, requiring that the rules be changed (as prescribed by Cantor and others). It is on the strength of this cheat that the infinitesimal calculus exists. For over a century, this has been officially rationalized to high school and college students using infinite converging series and the Cauchy-Weierstrass epsilon-delta technique. But on close examination, this fails to provide a satisfactory explanation of *either* infinitesimals *or* the calculus.

This situation has given rise to new mathematical perspectives and techniques including Lebesgue integration, nonstandard analysis, and pointless topology. The CTMU affords a new perspective of its own.

May 21, 2017

In natural sciences

143. Is mathematics unreasonably effective in the natural sciences?

Reality consists of patterned substance, i.e., substance which displays patterns through which it is recognized. "Pattern" is thus analogous to the syntax in terms of which a language is recognized by its users. Mathematics is a human formalization of the highest (most ubiquitous) level of this syntax, and thus describes reality and our recognition of it in a very general way.

As it presently exists, this formalization is not perfect; despite what one sometimes hears from self-congratulatory professional academics, the patterns which have thus far been formalized by human mathematicians are only imperfectly understood by them. However, mathematics can nonetheless be functionally defined as "the patterns through which we recognize our reality", thus circumventing the intellectual shortcomings of human mathematicians. This generic functional definition can then be trimmed using any special-purpose restrictions we might wish to apply in particular contexts.

When mathematics is defined in this way, its effectiveness in the natural sciences is no mystery at all; it is effective in the natural sciences precisely because it describes the syntax through which natural scientists identify reality. This relationship between reality and those who observe, study, and theorize about it is called a "supertautology", the structure of which requires that reality be modeled as a special kind of "language". This has all been formalized in a true "theory of everything" called the Cognitive Theoretic Model of the Universe (CTMU). The CTMU can be described as a metatheory of science, or if one prefers, as "(meta) mathematical metaphysics".

The CTMU has been the best-kept secret in the history of science and philosophy for the last thirty years or so. This is because it amounts to metaphysics, which many so-called experts absurdly regard as impossible despite their manifest inability to argue coherently against it. Thus, even though the CTMU was authored by a man widely described as the smartest in the world (Christopher Langan), it has been roundly ignored in what can only be described as a collective fit of academic spite and incomprehension.

December 24, 2017

P vs NP problem

144.   How close is Chris Langan to solving the P versus NP problem?

The matter has been satisfactorily resolved for my own purposes (which, incidentally, are the only purposes about which I care in this context).

There are two different solutions, one of which applies in a certain framework defined as "metacausal", "precomputational" or "protocomputational", and the other of which applies in a causal or computational limit thereof. This amounts to a relativization of the solution. Although I can't say for sure, I suspect that in the view of the "Millennium Prize" Committee, this falls short of an actual Y|N solution, leaving me nothing whatsoever to gain by submission.

(We also have the serious problem of bias on the Millennium Prize Committee, expressed by Andrew Wiles as their complete certainty that no non-academic is capable of solving any of the problems. This, of course, guarantees that the submissions of nonacademics will in effect be circular-filed, leaving them no rational choice but to disregard such prizes, and where necessary, the professional academics who award them to each other.)

February 14, 2018

Problem solving

145. Has it ever happened that an ordinary person found the solution to an unsolved mathematics problem?

Mathematically uneducated people have often found the solutions for previously unsolved logical and mathematical problems and puzzles. For example, the legendary Games columnist Martin Gardner credited many amateurs for the solutions of difficult math and logic puzzles published in *Scientific American*.

Although Academia, Inc. would like the public to believe otherwise – it is, after all, in business for profit – intelligence and ingenuity are innate human characteristics that cannot be bought and paid for at a university. A case can be made that some amount of academic training is all but necessary for the solution of certain very difficult mathematical problems, especially ones which cannot be understood (let alone solved) by the typical layman. But in the large, professional academics – who notoriously tend to fixate on just the problems salient within their personal specialties – do not have a monopoly on the selection or solution of "good" or interesting mathematical problems.

Historically, the intellectual penetration to formulate and solve really interesting problems of great import to the future intellectual and practical development of mankind came almost exclusively from formally untrained people, including those who laid the groundwork for modern disciplines which now reek of academic snobbery. Such people worked from first principles, an ability that professional academics, many of whom are weighted down with leaden orthodoxy, have forgotten how to use, recognize, and properly value.

September 7, 2018

Proving God's existence

146. Can mathematics tell if God exists?

Of course it can: the mere existence of mathematics suffices. Something is needed in order to distribute it as an ordered pattern over our entire domain of thought and experience, and it turns out that this "something" bears description as God. This can be couched in rock-hard mathematical language.

September 29, 2017

Pure mathematics

147. When will Chris Langan release a purely mathematical version of Christopher Langan's Cognitive-Theoretic Model of the Universe (CTMU)?

There is no "purely mathematical version" of anything with real-world meaning.

"Pure", uninterpreted, unapplied mathematics is devoid of external correspondence; no theory which consists exclusively of "pure mathematics" has real-world relevance. At the very least, definitions must be given which apply to the real world as well as to the mathematical structures themselves, along with an overall real-world correspondence (model).

As for the question "When will Chris Langan release a mathematical version of the CTMU?" (note the elimination of "purely"), I've already done this on several past occasions. Further mathematical descriptions are in the works, but must await proper venues for publication.

February 19, 2018

MEGA FOUNDATION

Operations

148. Is Chris Langan's Mega Foundation still active?

Absolutely. As a matter of fact, we have a large construction project in progress that is designed to facilitate and enhance our operations.

Unfortunately, the construction has been delayed by various errors and oversights on the parts of some of the contractors involved. We won't be able to make use of our new facilities until the problems are corrected, the construction project has been brought to a more advanced stage of completion, and we've brought in one or more volunteers to help with IT and physical maintenance.

Meanwhile, basic operations are continuous and ongoing, and we've tentatively scheduled a gathering for this autumn.

[By the way, the entire Mega Foundation website was placed on a secure platform two years ago in the expectation that the construction project would be complete and we could move forward again. The changes were quite extensive, but largely invisible to those visiting the site. As for the visible content of the site, it will change only if and when there is a need to change it. Additional content may of course be expected at some point.]

May 7, 2017

METAPHYSICS

Cosmology

149. What does the CTMU contribute to cosmology?

Cosmology, along with ontology and epistemology, began as a branch of metaphysics. Because the deepest issues in cosmology – the origin of the cosmos, accelerating cosmic expansion, the nature of causation, and so on – require a well-structured metaphysical metalanguage of physics for their proper formulation and solution, metaphysics is still where cosmology belongs.

This, of course, does not preclude the relevance of physical research to cosmology. Physics is more than welcome in cosmology, and has carved itself a very respectable niche in the field. Problems arise only when physics tries to steal the entire show, something which it is unequipped to do as a matter of logico-mathematical fact. The structure of physics simply doesn't allow it.

There is exactly one properly formulated theory of metaphysics: the CTMU. It follows that the CTMU must be credited with putting cosmology back where it belongs, and thereby making it possible to express and solve cosmological problems which do not admit of physical expression and solution.

July 14, 2018

Definition

150. What is metaphysics?

The proper definition of metaphysics has three escalating levels.

The body of theory which is "beyond physics". (This usage is due to Aristotle's "editor" Andronicus of Rhodes, who introduced the term to describe that part of Aristotle's explanation of reality which underlies physics.)

The field consisting of ontology, cosmology, and epistemology. In other words, the theory which deals with (a) the most general abstract proper-ties, *existence* and *nonexistence*, and all lesser properties subsumed by them; (b) the set of all substantive referents of those properties, namely the cosmos including all of its parts and aspects; and (c) the episte-mological (attributive, perceptual and/or cognitive) correspondence between the properties and their referents. (Note that these fields are not separable.)

A logically idempotent supertautological metalanguage of reality at large, defined in such a way as to coherently refer to reality, formulate ques-tions regarding it, and express answers for the questions. This meta-language is called the CTMU, short for *Cognitive Theoretic Model of the Universe*. The CTMU, which functions as its own universe and model, and which may be considered identical to the high-level structure of reality itself, is described elsewhere on this site.

I sympathize with those who throw up their hands at the idea of describ-ing an integrated discipline covering everything which has been called "metaphysics" over the years. In recognition of their difficulties, my own approach has been somewhat more limited: to educe a comprehensive reality-theoretic framework in which all valid physical and metaphys-ical concepts, relationships, and theories can be jointly interpreted or *modeled* in the logical sense. Due to this shift of focus, metaphysics now exists as a rigorous discipline which subsumes not only the empirical and mathematical sciences, but the humanities and religion as well.

February 13, 2018

Dyson, Freeman

151. What does Christopher Langan think about Freeman Dyson's metaphysics?

The CTMU is absolutely essential to the proper development of Freeman Dyson's "cosmic metaphysics of mind".

Dyson: "The universe shows evidence of the operations of mind on three levels. The first level is the level of elementary physical processes in quantum mechanics. Matter in quantum mechanics is [...] constantly making choices between alternative possibilities according to proba-bilistic laws. [...] The second level at which we detect the operations of mind is the level of direct human experience. [...] [I]t is reasonable to believe in the existence of a third level of mind, a mental component of the universe. If we believe in this mental component and call it God, then we can say that we are small pieces of God's mental apparatus" [*Infinite In All Directions* (1988), p. 297]

The CTMU can be described as the complete explication of this viewpoint, and more. This is interesting, as Professor Dyson and I must have been thinking very similar thoughts during the 1980's. The difference: Professor Dyson, who was very capable as a physicist but lacked the specific kinds of knowledge needed for the development of such metaphysical ideas, was a professional academic with full access to the academic monopoly which controls scholarly communication and intellectual commerce (hard publishing, electronic media, and so on).

I, on the other hand, lacked this advantage. So although I was vastly better able to develop such ideas, I was completely ignored by Professor Dyson and his academic colleagues. There is simply no way to compel these people to pay the slightest attention to anything emerging from the real world outside their vast institutional bubble, and unfortunately, compulsion is exactly what would have been required.

So much for the efficiency and integrity of academia as the self-styled vanguard of human intellectual progress. It simply doesn't work as advertised. Let's hope that something can finally be done about it.

May 19, 2018

Epistemology and ontology

152. What are some differences between epistemology and metaphysics?

There aren't any, other than being "different" aspects of the same thing. Epistemology cannot be separated from ontology, and ontology is squarely situated in metaphysics.

Why can't epistemology, the study of *knowledge and knowing*, be separated from ontology? Because knowledge *exists*, and existence is the subject matter of ontology.

Can metaphysics be regarded as "more general" than epistemology?

Not as long as metaphysics is about *knowing* and *being known as* "metaphysics".

Because each is an aspect or ingredient of the other, they are inseparable. This principle of inseparability amounts to *epistemological holism*, or if one prefers, *ontological* or *metaphysical* holism.

This kind of holism is central to the theory of mathematical metaphysics known as the **CTMU**, short for *Cognitive Theoretic Model of the Universe*.

The CTMU is by far the most advanced theory of metaphysics in existence.

June 7, 2018

Framework of reality

153.   What is the purpose of Metaphysics?

Where metaphysics describes every aspect of the existence, intelligibility, origin, structure, and dynamics *of* reality *for* reality, it *equates to* reality, and its purpose is therefore that of reality itself. That is, its purpose is to provide reality with an ontological, epistemological, and cosmological framework supporting the existence, intelligibility, origin, structure, and dynamics of reality.

Where *science* is a real process that reveals the nature of reality to and for the inhabitants of reality itself, metaphysics includes science in its descriptive framework and thus qualifies as "metascience". In other words, it is the discipline by virtue of which science is rendered self-explanatory, and its purpose can be understood accordingly.

May 13, 2018

Metalogical system

154.   What is the relationship of metaphysics to logic and epistemology?

Metaphysics is best understood as a metalogical system, the CTMU, which matches the overall structure of reality, and in which it is therefore possible to describe and model reality in its entirety. In other words, it equates to a comprehensive higher-level extension of logic, where *logic* is the syntax of 2-valued identification and therefore integral to epistemology. Thus, logic and epistemology are inseparable aspects of metaphysics. They're all part of an inseparable whole.

May 27, 2018

Metaphysical metalanguage

155. What is metaphysics according to Christopher Langan's Cognitive-Theoretic Model of the Universe (CTMU)?

According to the CTMU, metaphysics is a unique explanatory metalanguage of physics with certain mathematical properties that have been explored in various papers and essays which are readily available online.

February 9, 2018

Philosophy

156. What is the relationship between metaphysics and philosophy?

Traditionally, metaphysics has been regarded as a branch of philosophy which coexists with other branches of the philosophical tree. This amounts to a loose and simplistic definition of *metaphysics* as the application of *philosophical methods* – systematic inquiry through the use of reason, rational argumentation, and critical discussion – to fundamental *metaphysical issues* typically including first principles, ultimate origins and ends, being, knowledge, substance, causation, space, time, and identity.

However, a bit of reflection suffices to reveal a problem with the supposed proper inclusion of metaphysics in philosophy: just as philosophical methodology is so general that it distributes over (includes) metaphysics, the metaphysical issues enumerated above are so general that they apply to philosophy in its entirety. In short, philosophy and metaphysics are inseparable; the content of metaphysics cannot be rationally disentangled from the methodology of philosophy or vice versa.

Now here's another eye-opener: science and mathematics both began as philosophy, and the pairing of philosophy and metaphysics continues to apply to them with full force. So ultimately, all of these fields must be considered together.

The suppression of this epistemological holism by way of sloppy semantics and academic compartmentalization is artificial and strictly illusory.

May 5, 2018

Physics

157.   What is the connection between physics and metaphysics?

Metaphysics is a metalanguage relating the theoretical object language of physics to the physical (empirical, observable) universe; it expresses a model-theoretic relationship between them. Owing to the mathematical structure of the metalanguage (implied by ontological closure and related criteria), physical reality – a coupling of physical theory and observational data – can be understood as the "observational limit" of an inclusive metaphysical reality described by the metalanguage. The metaphysical metalanguage which describes this all-inclusive metaphysical reality is a mathematical theory of metaphysics called the *Cognitive Theoretic Model of the Universe (CTMU)*.

May 2, 2018

Scope of metaphysics

158.   Does metaphysics entail anything that is not empirical, and if so, is theoretical physics and for example the theory of relativity considered metaphysics?

Well, that all depends, doesn't it.

Let "physical reality" consist of that which is directly and replicably perceptible, plus all that can be directly logically inferred from it. This definition depends on the meaning of *logical inference*, with the burden on anyone claiming that inobservables have been "logically inferred" to specify the logical system in which the inferences have been made.

Almost every physical advance in history has adjoined to the existing version of "physics" new inobservable concepts and quantities that could not be strictly deduced within any system then recognizable as *logic*, or within an axiomatic system known to be universal. Instead, they were empirically induced from particular observations in order to relate and explain them *without certainty*. Where the burden of logical proof has never been met, such advances cannot yet be pronounced physical.

But are they metaphysical? That depends on how *metaphysics* is defined. Where it is defined as the "deep structure of reality" and formulated as a consistent comprehensive metalanguage in which all valid physical constructs and theories can be expressed, related, analyzed, compared, and modeled – as it is defined in the CTMU – the answer is *yes*, provided that the theoretical advance is itself correct and logically valid within its domain. But where the theory is not a valid limit or subtheory of metaphysics, or where the wrong definition of metaphysics is in force, the answer is *no*.

In other words, to the extent that physical theories with inobservable components, such as both GR and QM (General Relativity and Quantum Mechanics), are correct, they are metaphysics under the most powerful definition of metaphysics (that of the CTMU). But under a weaker definition incapable of actually containing reality, one may be limited to saying merely that they are "partially nonphysical".

In either case, such theories are not merely physical.

May 27, 2018

MULTIPLEX UNITY

Coherent interconnection

159. Can someone elaborate on how the MU principle relates to the "problem" of Unity and Multiplicity in the CTMU? How does MU defines the relationship between the two?

In the CTMU, the Principle of Multiplex Unity – which can be simplistically expressed, in the language of John Archibald Wheeler, as "one universe out of many" – explains how reality coheres despite consisting of many parts which appear to be separate and largely independent of each other. In the 2002 paper *The Cognitive Theoretic Model of the Universe: A New Kind of Reality Theory*, it is a well-defined mathematical concept explicitly related to dual forms of inclusion. It is strongly related to the CTMU concepts *syndiffeonesis* and *supertautology*.

Without the MU Principle, there would be no way to coherently interconnect our many "subjective universes" – or if one prefers, the set of scientific observers and frames of reference – in one common reality.

February 18, 2018

MUSK, ELON

Evaluating utility

160. Who is more valuable to humanity, Chris Langan, who claims
      proof of god, or Elon Musk, businessman, who tries to secure
      power by presenting a good image and expanding his portfolio?

Let's have a rational look at this question, shall we?

Just so no one gets confused, let's make it as simple as possible. Take
a socio-economic system X, and two people A and B within it. Suppose
that A is a corporate CEO who has never actually invented or discovered anything (but managed to attract a lot of favorable attention from
venture capitalists and investment bankers), and that B is a person who
has weathered a lot of adversity in order to bring humankind a new
worldview (no one who actually understands anything about the CTMU
denies that it is both original and insightful, and in any case, I could
easily crush anyone who denies it were I so disposed).

As we all know, value and scarcity are very closely related. The scarcer
something is, the more valuable it is. CEO's are a dime a dozen, and so
are salesmen who can attract a lot of favorable attention from venture
capitalists and investment bankers. In fact, they've become annoyingly
common, and even worse, we seem to have more of them every day.
Clearly, such people are only as valuable as they are irreplaceable. But
if techie billionaires/corporate CEO's were ever irreplaceable, this is no
longer the case. Any one of them can be replaced by any other; they all
cherry-pick whatever experts they might need from Academia, Inc., and
delegate all of the real intellectual responsibility to their employees. And
as if that weren't enough, their positive value exists only with respect to
the system X in which their social utility is defined; if X happens to be
displacing a better system, then their true value is negative.

It follows that their comparative human worth is strictly limited, and
the burden of proof is on anyone who claims that there aren't a million
others out there who could step into their shoes and rake in the loot
just as well as they do.

Do you see where this is going yet? ;)

January 6, 2018

Outlier or not

161. Based on the book written by Malcolm Gladwell, would Elon
      Musk also be defined as an Outlier?

Well, yes and no.

Any billionaire is an "outlier" with respect to the overall distribution of
wealth. In addition, we can probably say that Elon began with somewhat
less wealth, and more initiative, than did the average billionaire. We
can even say that Elon is considerably "luckier" than others, insofar as
certain things came together for Elon that would not necessarily have
come together for another person, in another place, at another time.

However, those who insist that Elon is a "genius" have their work cut out
for them. Elon has never been an inventor or discoverer of new concepts,
and as far as most of us are aware, has never really exerted himself for
any cause or reason that did not promise to result in the further bloating
of his personal bank balance. Thus, he is not an outlier with respect to
his motives, which are every bit as materialistic and self-interested as
those of any other businessman.

January 14, 2018

Productivity

162. Will Elon Musk study the CTMU and thus turn into a productive
      member of society?

I have no idea whether Elon Musk is even aware of the CTMU. However,
the fact that he is reputed to be a convicted atheist suggests that the
CTMU is not on his list of preferred reading material.

I have never said, and would not say, that Elon Musk is not "a productive
member of society". I would merely point out that the uniqueness and
long-term value of his contributions has not yet been determined.

There is another answer on this page which, itself and in its comments section, contains several factually incorrect and/or pejorative statements or insinuations regarding me and the CTMU. As its comments are now disabled – which raises the question of how any comments got there in the first place – and lest the author's personal opinion be mistaken by the unwary for the official stance of Quora, I'll take this opportunity to include a few corrections.

If there is a CTMU/Langan "advertising ploy in action", I have nothing to do with it. I've posted only one question on Quora, and it was merely a duplicate of a previous question which had been erased by the OP along with my answer (this could ostensibly be verified by the Quora IT department, although I have no idea how one would make that happen). I have never instructed anyone, either publicly or privately, to post any questions whatsoever about me or my work on this site or any other.

I have never said that "If Elon Musk doesn't believe in this [CTMU] theory then he isn't a productive member of society, and ... is going to hell."

I have never said that "every single other person [out of "billions of people"] who doesn't believe in this theory" is unproductive and therefore going to hell. I have no idea where this strange notion originated.

It is erroneous of the author to assume that "if she continue[s] to see such questions, [she] will know [her] theory is correct – that this is nothing more than a cloaked advertising campaign going on." Such questions could just as well be generated by honest interest in the CTMU. (After all, several academic papers have been published on it.)

It is not necessarily true that "Something that is truth and sincere is not promoted Anonymously." In fact, the truth value of a theory or assertion is independent of who promotes it or how.

It is not true that "[The CTMU] never went anywhere for no one really took it seriously." My CTMU papers have been downloaded hundreds of thousands if not millions of times, and attracted many sincere followers.

The author links to an extremely contemptuous and pejorative screed by another Quora participant claiming to be a "physicist" or a student of physics. This screed was duly collapsed long ago by Quora Moderation. She has attempted to "uncollapse it" by linking to it in a comment, prompting others to read it. This clearly opposes the attempt of Quora Moderation to quarantine it.

[**Addendum**: The person responsible for generating all of the above errors has apparently modified her original answer to assert that Quora never collapsed the misleading and aggressively disparaging answer of the so-called "physicist" she cites. Yet I still find it to have been collapsed, as I have found it since around the time the alleged "physicist" lost an argument with me in its comments section and had all of my comments (and possibly also my own answer to the question) collapsed or totally removed. So either the "physicist's" answer was collapsed as I've stated, or Quora is collapsing different answers for different people.]

That should do it for now. I hope I've dispelled or at least reduced any confusion that may have existed with regard to the above issues.

January 27, 2018

PETERSON, JORDAN

Debate invitation

163. Does Jordan Peterson regard the CTMU as a metamathematical, logically rigorous scientific theory of metaphysics?

God help poor Jordan if he ever says otherwise! (I'm afraid he wouldn't stand much of a chance against me, and as a North American clinical psychologist, he probably knows it.)

Of course, maybe someone doubts this who actually knows Jordan. If so, then have Jordan give me a call and we'll see about setting something up. I'm awfully busy, but if he's polite and respectful, there won't be a problem.

September 30, 2018

Worldview assessment

164. What does Chris Langan think about Jordan B. Peterson?

I think that in some ways, Jordan's heart is in the right place — he displayed courage in taking his stance on the issue of compulsory speech (at least with respect to gender pronouns, if not necessarily all aspects of PC doctrine).

However, it occurs to me that although Jordan is clearly intelligent and well-spoken, his personal history as a lifelong professional academic is bound to have limited his experience outside the Ivory Tower while exposing him to intensive indoctrination, and this may have limited his ideological flexibility and real-world awareness. For example, he seems to labor under the delusion that we inhabit a real meritocracy in which strong, upstanding "alpha males" are rewarded for merit and always get the girl. (That's just not how it works out here in the real world.)

It also strikes me that Jordan may be overextending himself by staking claims on difficult intellectual territory, including theology, religion, morality, and other metaphysically loaded fields. As a North American clinical psychologist with much to say about intelligence and intelligence testing, he has in all likelihood encountered my name. Yet, like academics everywhere, he shows no sign of knowing that I and the CTMU exist, and thus seems to think that his rather pedestrian views on certain metaphysical issues are state-of-the-art.

This being understood, I wish Jordan well. I'd merely suggest that if he really wants to be on the bleeding edge, he'll need to widen his acknowledgement of expertise and authority beyond the opaque, sweating walls of the academic hothouse. As always, out here in reality-land is where it's really happening.

June 12, 2018

PHILOSOPHY

Arrogation by Academia

165.   What are the shortcomings of philosophy?

The major shortcoming of philosophy is that it has been arrogated by Academia, Inc., which functions like an intellectual trade union / pyramidal growth economy / Ponzi-style credentialization scam with membership standards irrelevant to the content of philosophy and for that matter intellectual merit. Because Academia has been corporatized and therefore tightly standardized, and because its socialization and indoctrination functions have come to outweigh its traditional education function, it now enforces a rigid philosophical narrative based on PC doctrine. This kind of ideological standardization is diametrically opposed to free intellectual inquiry and intellectual balance and integrity. As a result, the phrase "modern philosopher" is now all but oxymoronic. The typical modern philosopher, or at least one who commands recognition as such, is a professional academic who cannot think independently, who lives in abject fear of losing his/her job for deviating from institutional orthodoxy (or saying boo to an administrator), and who wouldn't know a worthwhile philosophical framework if it crashed the stage on live television, bit him on the nose, and yanked his undies down around his knees. This is why physicists and other scientists have been eating philosophy's lunch for the last few decades with total impunity, "bitch-slapping" the discipline around the block virtually at will.

October 2, 2016

Cartesian mind-body dualism

166. Do you agree with Chris Langan that Cartesian mind-body dualism fails because both mind and body, in any such theoretical separation, are still being discussed through one syntax (i.e. English), thus showing that the two are in the same reality?

WARNING: This question is badly garbled. Specifically, the restriction of cognitive syntax to one particular natural language has nothing to do with the CTMU or anything else I've ever said or written.

In fact, there is no way to cogently disagree with the CTMU. In particular, the simultaneous recognition of mind and body implies that they share common structure, and this precludes absolute dualism. There is not a logician or philosopher on Earth who can coherently argue otherwise.

Now to the issue of why the wording of this question is so badly skewed. Questions like this are the work of trolls; that much is clear. The real issue is whether the readership of Quora is sufficiently stupid and malevolent to regularly turn such trolling into a pretext for badmouthing people and issues about which most of its members know precisely nothing, or merely into an opportunity to slip in a snide jab or two in order to boost personal self-esteem at the expense of truth.

Some of the answers here aren't that bad. But still, Quora has been failing this test, and those who have contributed pejorative answers here are among the reasons. There is nothing positive that can be said about such people; they are gulls and suckers, and they are evidently too dull and witless to stop themselves from being played like yoyos.

My advice to the gullible: don't make a fool of yourself. Even when a troll pushes your buttons because they stick up a mile, exercise a little self-control and refrain from slavishly indulging your impulse to spew resentment and illogic. Quora is not supposed to be anyone's personal hatefest.

Thanks for your attention.

August 16, 2018

Chris Langan and Immanuel Kant

167. Is Chris Langan the Immanuel Kant of our era?

Only in the sense that the CTMU, which has comprised the sum total of (competent) mathematical metaphysics for the last three or so decades, is the ultimate extension of some of Kant's more perspicuous reasoning, transplanted into a vastly richer and more sophisticated conceptual environment. However, Kant made certain errors which the CTMU does not replicate, e.g., regarding the noumenon-phenomenon distinction. Thus, the CTMU is precisely what Kantian philosophy has consistently failed to produce: a comprehensive, self-consistent ontology and global conceptual framework supporting the entirety of human knowledge.

February 18, 2018

Harris, Sam

168. Sam Harris says the sense of self is an illusion, that we're just our brains, the ego doesn't exist. Does the CTMU agree with this claim?

No, the CTMU does not support the claims that "the sense of self is an illusion, that we're just our brains, [and] the ego doesn't exist."

From a CTMU perspective, these claims are ridiculous, and in my opinion, Mr. Harris wouldn't have a chance of prevailing against me in an argument about it. (As this is one of those threads that was already packed with misinformation by the time I got here, I'll just leave it at that for now. Suffice it to say that of the answers below, only one – by Joe Moyenne – contains so much as a single accurate statement about my work.)

April 29, 2018

Hume, David

169.   What is David Hume's analysis and criticism of causality?

Basically, that **one cannot in general directly observe or logically deduce a causal connection**. One can observe a sequence of events and hopefully label it a "cause-effect relationship", but without logical implication, the label is merely a token of optimism; mere statistical confirmation proves nothing. This is called the "problem of induction" and permeates the empirical sciences, theories of which usually fall well short of logical implication or entailment. No matter how loudly an empirical scientist may proclaim that "The empirical evidence proves theory X!", proof is simply not possible within the constraints of empirical methodology.

May 10, 2018

Philosophy of physics

170.   What do physicists think of the philosophers of physics who philosophize about physics?

If we're talking about *competent* philosophers of physics (or of science in general), roughly the same thing that the foxes guarding the henhouse think of the farmer pointing a shotgun at them. ;)

May 26, 2018

Prevalence of physicalism

171.   What do philosophers think of Chris Langan's CTMU?

That all depends on the philosopher.

Most modern philosophers, particularly those of the academic variety, have been abjectly cowed by the relative success of the hard sciences, which – although they have not imparted the deep understanding of the overall structure of reality that they once seemed to promise – have nevertheless resulted in quite a lot of impressive and often very profitable gadgetry. Accordingly, ever cognizant of what is good for their academic careers, they subscribe to (metaphysical or methodological) naturalism.

Naturalism, which amounts to physicalism or physical monism, is the dominant worldview among academicians, especially those in the hard sciences. Because the hard sciences are where the corporate profiteers of Academia, Inc. butter their bread, academic philosophers stick to it like glue, at least where the rubber meets the road. That is, they confine their philosophical meanderings within the boundaries of physicalism, merely fleshing out its details while studiously ignoring any academic outsider who might have a better way.

Obviously, physicalism – which is strongly associated with various so-called "naturalistic" ideologies like atheism, secularism, and communism – is not valid from a CTMU standpoint, and the CTMU is therefore summarily rejected by the proponents of these belief systems.

In contrast, some philosophers have managed to retain three things once considered essential to success in philosophy: an open mind, high intelligence, and an understanding of the technical aspects of metaphysical philosophy as it relates to conventional scientific theories as object-languages. Within this group, those familiar with the CTMU are almost universally in favor of it.

One can only wish that there were more of them around. ;)

[**Addendum**: One of the answers in this thread, written by someone absurdly claiming to have a degree in "philosophy", is highly erroneous. Unfortunately, when I posted a warning about this in its comments section, it was immediately deleted and comments were closed. Accordingly, I'm repeating the warning here.

"**WARNING**: I'm the author of the CTMU, and this answer contains nothing that can be recognized as having anything to do with it. In addition to ironic insults involving "word salad" and "masturbation", it consists of a quote of which the critic professes complete incomprehension; a handful of terms taken out of context and mistakenly interpreted as synonyms of "circular or self-referential"; and erroneous descriptions of the CTMU as "perception and thought is reality" and "the claims of the theory are proven by the claims of the theory." As these errors are misleading at best and malicious at worst, readers are hereby advised to ignore this answer in its entirety. Thank you for your attention."

Answers like the one which occasioned this warning do not come from philosophers, but from trolls, and any upvotes or endorsements that they receive are from other trolls. Remember, not everyone who represents himself as a "philosopher" has the intellectual wherewithal and understanding to engage in philosophy, and many of those who do not are given to venting their resentment of those who do in unkind and misleading ways. Forewarned is forearmed.]

August 9, 2018

PHYSICS

Force of gravity

172. If you couldn't feel the force of gravity, would the directions of up, down, left, and right still exist?

Yes. There would still exist 3 linearly independent spatial dimensions which, when reversed, yield 6 directions (up, down; left, right; forward, backward). But rather than being defined with respect to an observer standing on the surface of a gravitating body or oriented with respect to an external center of mass, they would be defined with respect to the observer alone. Where you're the observer, up and down would run from the center of your body toward your head and your feet respectively; left and right would run outward through your left and right sides respectively; and forward and backward would run outward to your front and rear respectively. In other words, your body would define a 3D coordinate system with axes lying along the lines of intersection of three anatomical planes: sagittal, coronal, and transverse.

September 17, 2017

Hawking, Stephen

173. Will there be a discussion between old Stephen Hawking and Chris Langan anytime soon?

ABC News reportedly tried to set up a meeting between me and Hawking in the late 1990's. (They asked me and I agreed.) Unfortunately, it turned out that Hawking was surrounded by academic flunkies who carefully screened all of his invitations, and they (apparently) screened me out.

Oh, well. *C'est la vie.*

January 14, 2018

Indispensability of logic

174. Can you have absolute proof of anything in physics, or is it all
a case of having theories?

Of course you can.

I see a great deal of insistent yammering here about how nothing can be
proven in the empirical sciences. That's true for the empirical sciences
minus logic; proof is a logical operation, and is therefore a matter of logic
rather than empirical induction. The problem, of course, is that logic is
a very high-level science in its own right, and minus logic, there is no
such thing as science at all (including physics).

Logic is the onboard "scientific master theory" that you are given when
you are placed into the world and issued a brain, and it permanently
holds the upper hand over all other scientific theories. Logic distributes
over the empirical and mathematical sciences in the sense that as soon
as a logical inconsistency arises in any of them, logic demands either
that it be immediately resolved, or that the operative theory be deemed
incorrect and repaired no matter how long it may take. This applies no
matter where or how the inconsistency arises. Thus, science is never in
a position to reject that which can be logically derived from logic itself ...
e.g., from propositional tautologies like "x or not-x" (and there are other
kinds of logical tautology as well).

The question thus comes down to whether or not any observable fact
can be tautologically deduced, given that logic applies on the level of
observation itself, with observability critically depending on logical
truth-valuation. In particular, given any scientific observation or exper-
iment, it must be true rather than false that one is making a replicable,
scientifically valid observation, with everyone agreeing on what has
been observed (this scientific criterion is called *replicability*). As logic
is just the mathematical structure of truth, this automatic invocation
of truth amounts to an automatic invocation of logic.

There is a certain naive (and absurd) viewpoint according to which scientifically relevant tautological inference is forever impossible. However,
none of those espousing this viewpoint can prove it. The amazing fact
here – the scientific elephant in the room – is that although the Scientific
Method is basically a model-theoretic application of logic, most scientists fail to understand the mathematical logic that governs model theory.

In fact, they can't even shake a stick in its direction, largely because much of it is new. Rather, they merely understand certain assumptions that fed into the smattering of logic that they were forced to learn in school.

It follows that asking the typical scientist what can ultimately be proven in the sciences is at best a waste of time, and at worst highly misleading. The game that scientists are trained to play is empirical induction, not advanced logic, and this is a fact from which they cannot escape. Some of them are quite good at plain old empirical induction – that's why science works! – but this is not to be mistaken for deep logical penetration and self-awareness on the parts of most scientists. That, unfortunately, remains a faraway pipe dream.

January 28, 2018

Particles in CTMU

175. What are atoms and other particles in the CTMU theory of Chris Langan?

In the CTMU, fermions (particles obeying the Pauli Exclusion Principle) are *syntactic operators*, quantum identities capable of mutual interaction. (These identities are called "syntactic operators" because they operate on each other according to the syntax of a certain language that couples with the manifold in which they exist, and in which other particles are defined on them.)

January 14, 2018

Physicists and CTMU

176. Why don't physicists accept the CTMU? The CTMU is a far superior theory of reality than any physics theory.

What on Earth would give anyone the idea that "physicists don't accept the CTMU"? This assumption is simply false.

Admittedly, many physicists *haven't heard* of the CTMU, largely because it's outside their specialties. (Physics has been pretty well carved up over the years.) But in just the last week, I've corresponded with three major physicists, one a Nobel Prize winner. Yet another famous physicist, John Wheeler, inventor of the phrase "black hole", actually *liked* it – he told me so around twenty years ago.

You know, this rabid anti-CTMU trolling has to stop, if only because it's making this whole website look ten kinds of ridiculous. There's not a "physicist" on this site – or a physics *troll*, for that matter, which is what some Quora "physics experts" seem to be – whom I couldn't pretty much mangle, intellectually speaking, if he/she tried to debunk or discredit it.

A little less of this nonsense, if you wouldn't mind.

September 20, 2018

Wheeler, John

177. Does Chris Langan have any evidence for his claim that John Wheeler liked the CTMU?

Yes, I do. Specifically, I still have one of Wheeler's personalized illustrated postcards on which he had penned a request that I meet with him at Princeton (unfortunately, I was unable to get away from any of the three or so jobs I had at the time).

The next time I see it around the office, I'll scan it and post a copy somewhere. Until then, any doubters may feel free to doubt it as much as they like, as I really couldn't care less.

September 29, 2018

POLITICS

Gun control

178. What would likely happen if suddenly there were no more presumptive questions posed on Quora about the suspension of the 2nd amendment and suddenly everyone is happily turning in their guns? Would life on Quora be forever changed?

Governments are by far the most prolific mass murderers in history, amounting in many cases to an especially brutal form of organized crime. Other mass murderers pale into insignificance by comparison.

The Second Amendment of the US Constitution equates to a US citizen's right of self-defense against the government. Without it, the wholesale murder of citizens would begin as soon as the government, possessing a virtual monopoly on the efficient application of deadly force, deemed it advantageous.

In that case, Quora would indeed change. Everyone would be anxiously parroting the official narrative on everything, just in order to avoid that pounding on the door in the middle of the night.

Don't even ask why this is so hard for some people to understand – it would only get them started. Idiocy is never to be encouraged.

[**Addendum**: It has sometimes been argued that mere guns leave citizens powerless against a government with military weaponry at its disposal. But governments tend to avoid the use of tanks, planes, and bombs against their people because this would involve the destruction of property, and governments consist of venal and corrupt individuals who generally prefer theft to destruction. The object is usually to kill or incarcerate people while stealing their money and possessions, which requires that armed agents be sent out against them ... uniformed flunkies who must worry about being shot by those whose property they are stealing under cover of law.

As the idea is usually to make a few high-profile examples so that everyone else will meekly hand over their money and possessions on demand, official acts of theft tend to occur in isolation. Guns can be quite effective in deterring amoral government thugs who would otherwise confiscate one's private property under asset forfeiture laws, auction off one's home for nonpayment of oppressive taxes, appropriate one's land under "eminent domain", take one's children in retaliation for home-schooling or refusing to vaccinate them, arrest one for political crimes or "hate speech", etc. And of course, guns can also be effective in defending oneself and one's family against criminals and wild animals, a basic human right if ever there was one.

Government officials who steal with pen and paper are for the most part a cowardly lot who rightly fear revenge for their depredations. Maintaining an armed citizenry is an absolute necessity of keeping them honest, which would otherwise be impossible given their innate criminal propensities. These days, the option to abuse their power for personal advantage is what makes most bureaucrats and politicians tick – no matter how ethical and public-spirited they pretend to be, it's always in the back (if not the front) of their minds. When it comes down to them versus the little people, their prime imperative is always to come out on top.

Sadly, this is the nature of the governmental beast. It jealously exercises a virtual power monopoly not to keep us free and safe, but to protect its own privilege and secure itself from those at whose expense it exists. Forewarned is forearmed.]

October 11, 2017

179. Why are both sides of the gun issue so at odds with each other? Can't both sides come to table and compromise?

In the sentence "The right of the people to keep and bear Arms shall not be infringed," the phrase "shall not be infringed" greatly limits compromise. Beyond a certain point, gun control laws infringe on the right of private citizens to bear arms by delaying, obstructing, or denying their efforts to exercise that right, thus simply violating the Amendment.

Remember, a "right" is something that everyone either has from birth or has the opportunity to earn. Historically, the "opportunity to earn" this particular right – which the Founding Fathers considered an absolute necessity given the known tendency of governments to abuse the defenseless – has taken the form of, e.g., hunting safety courses and bans on gun ownership by those with criminal convictions involving gun violence against their fellow citizens. Aside from these rules, almost all proposed gun control legislation amounts to infringement.

History and current events show that any move to compromise with the political Left on the issue of gun control simply causes it to grab whatever minor short-term advantages might become available, and immediately issue new and more stringent demands. It has thus become increasingly clear that the Left has no intention of compromising on such matters, and that its anti-gun caterwauling is only reinforced and amplified by each small advantage that it gains.

As lasting, worthwhile agreement is clearly impossible to achieve under these circumstances, and legal attacks on the Second Amendment of the United States Constitution are extremely dangerous to the security and welfare of American citizens, politicians bent on attacking it should be democratically removed from office ... and so, unfortunately, should those who cave into their demands for the sake of "compromise".

April 5, 2018

Identity politics

180.   What is Chris Langan's view on identity politics?

My view on identity politics is that it can be justified only if everyone of any ethnicity is entitled to participate, in which case it is necessary for all (because failing to assert it, as when White people of European ancestry fail to assert it lest they be branded as "racists", means leaving oneself and one's group defenseless against competition for resources and opportunity). Alternatively, lest any group be denied its identity while others assert their own, group identity must be equitably denied to everyone.

Human identity is stratified, and thus has both individual and group levels. Accordingly, we can (and sometimes must) reason in terms of group identity. But when group self-identification is officially granted to some groups yet denied to others against which they compete, this can only result in imbalance and injustice. For example, when some overpopulating groups which have overtaxed their own resources by reproductive incontinence and homegrown oligarchy are allowed to migrate into the sovereign territories of worldwide ethnic minorities – e.g., people of European descent – and enjoy special "oppressed" status whereby they reap special benefits such as free food, free housing, free education, free healthcare, affirmative action, reproductive subsidies, and special treatment under the law, and are even credited with moral superiority due to their alleged "oppression", this can result in the destruction of the national, cultural, and ethnic identity of the hosts, leading ultimately to their extinction. Incoming groups which assert their own collective identities while denying their hosts any reciprocal right of political group cohesion thus amount to noxious, invasive, and ultimately lethal socioeconomic parasites. Obviously, any governmental authority which enforces or encourages such asymmetry – e.g., the European Union – is illegitimate.

Bear in mind that once we cease to treat individuals as individuals *per se*, thus allowing members of their respective groups to assert their ethnic, cultural, or religious (etc.) identities against their "oppressors", their group properties and statistics are automatically opened to scrutiny and comparative analysis. For example, if after several generations of special treatment in the educational sphere (compulsory school integration, special programs, modifications of educational procedure, racially defined college admission preferences, etc.), a particular "oppressed" group fails as a whole to outgrow these measures, its members are no longer entitled to exemption from objective characterization in terms of associated group statistics; if one wants to enjoy the social benefits attending ethically loaded group-defined properties like "belonging to an oppressed group", one must submit to rational policies formed on the basis of not just individual assessment, but empirically confirmed group-defined properties such as "belonging to a group exhibiting a relatively low mean IQ and a tendency to violently disrupt the educational environment". Continuing to pursue racially parameterized measures of human worth and achievement can only lead to personal injustice, social degradation, and biological degeneration (because such measures inevitably supplant any rational form of social, economic, and reproductive selection).

In short, identity politics should either be shut down immediately, or the majority populations of Europe and North America should be encouraged to assert their own ethnic and cultural identities and group interests with full force. Any governmental, academic, religious, or media authority which tries to prevent it is clearly unworthy of respect and obedience.

[**Note**: This answer has been "collapsed" on the supposed grounds that it "needs attribution". However, it absolutely *does not* need attribution, because it consists of my opinion on identity politics expressed entirely in my own original words as formed on the basis of my own original reasoning. The "collapse" has been appealed, so again we have a test of Quora and its moderation staff. If you have found this answer in a state of "collapse", it follows that Quora has once again failed the test.]

May 29, 2018

PSYCHOLOGY

Psychological disorders

181.   Why do psychopaths and narcissists manipulate differently?

Narcissism and psychopathy are personality disorders. There are many personality disorders, and they can and usually do overlap. Various disorders give rise to various structural and causational theories which purportedly describe them, and these theories may be mutually exclusive. But it would be a mistake to assume that the disorders themselves must necessarily follow suit. In principle, there is no reason why narcissism and psychopathy cannot overlap.

Often, the best that one can do after identifying a given subject's personal spectrum of psychological traits and disorders is to ask how much of each is exhibited, and how they might interact in various kinds of situation. After deciding on a specific proportion or psychological profile, one can then try to predict the person's cognitive and behavioral tendencies as a function of these traits and disorders in a given context. But of course, this can be hit or miss.

If one looks closely at the socioeconomic elite, for example, one finds a raft of characteristic personality disorders which free those who possess them from psychological constraints and inhibitions, like empathy, compassion, honesty, and morality, which might have impeded their progress toward material success. Obviously, the successful landlord cannot be so compassionate that he can't evict a poor family in the middle of winter if that's what it takes to save his business; the corporate climber cannot be so fair and honest that she never takes credit for the work of underlings (insofar as those lower down the ladder are often the ones doing all the intellectual and physical work); and the successful financier cannot be so empathic that he becomes paralyzed when he must yield to his "killer instinct" and knife his competition, or his clients, in the chest or in the back.

Narcissism and psychopathy both work to disinhibiting effect. For example, psychopathy helps suspend empathy so that one can objectify and manipulate those who might get in one's way, while narcissism frees one from compunction by inflating one's sense of entitlement and justification (one has succeeded because one is "really better" than those whom one has surpassed, or because one is so "lovable" that one's success is a matter of sheer popular consensus). Naturally, the winners of the race for wealth and power tend to enjoy a powerful combination of these "advantages". (We're not just picking on the wealthy and powerful alone, by the way; it just so happens that they lend themselves to the discussion by displaying a characteristic personality spectrum which has always been problematical for the rest of society precisely because its ill effects are amplified by the wealth and power with which it corre-lates. We could just as easily have focused on street criminals, whose ill effects on society tend to be more localized.)

Different personality disorders may be triggered by different situa-tions in various combinations, and the emotions which arise and the strategies employed may vary accordingly. The notion that the set of narcissists and the set of psychopaths are necessarily disjoint, and that one can always tell to which set a person belongs by his/her attitudes, strategies, and tactics, is simply inaccurate. The same person can act like a narcissist one minute and a psychopath or sociopath the next, or even like both at once, mixing and switching behaviors in largely unpredictable ways.

Such is the marvelous complexity of human psychology.

January 8, 2017

182. How do you reconcile the loss of identity (dementia for instance) with the existence of a personal God within Christopher Langan's Cognitive-Theoretic Model of the Universe (CTMU)?

Dementia is a "loss of memory", not of identity. Its symptoms include memory difficulties, but not a change or lapse of identity (provided that "identity" is not superficially and improperly defined on memories alone).

Dementia patients can be lucid provided that they can engage with physical reality and are thereafter "held in the moment" – they can tell stories, play cards, and so on. But when the context changes, their memory problems prevent them from keeping track of what they were just doing and/or thinking, and this "discontinuity in the narrative" can be mistaken by others for discontinuity of identity.

Provided that their condition is not complicated by an independent dissociative disorder, dementia patients typically experience no lapse or transformation of conscious identity as their symptoms come and go. This is due to the fact that human identity exists on a level of coherence that is independent of any particular context or narrative.

This is fully consistent with the CTMU concept of identity as formulated within that of Ultimate Reality or "God".

January 31, 2018

183. Can SCSPL from Christopher Langan's Cognitive-Theoretic Model of the Universe (CTMU) explain or map psychosis/schizophrenia and other mental health phenomena?

Of course it can. The CTMU isn't called the *"Cognitive* Theoretic Model of the Universe" for nothing.

The discipline of psychology began with metaphysics. Initially, before it was overpowered by physicalism and behaviorism, psychology permitted the consideration of mind without insisting that it be supervened entirely on matter. In contrast to the "naturalism" in terms of which modern psychology is understood, its older and more primitive theory even included mention of supernatural entities like angels and demons, and sometimes weird diagnoses and treatments to go along with them.

But then came the Age of Reason, and eventually, a complete reversal. Instead of remaining a spiritual being, man came to be interpreted in a mechanistic model of self according to which a human being is nothing but a machine ... a classical-mechanical automaton driven by self-interest and governed by impersonal laws of nature and rules of behaviorism, subject to conditioning on the basis of individual utility as defined on the pursuit of pleasure, the avoidance of pain, and biological standards of "fitness" including survival and reproduction. As for *mind*, it was pretty much reduced to *brain*.

But another reversal is now at hand, and everything is poised to come full circle. Physicalism has gone bankrupt, standing in embarrassed silence before the great metaphysical conundrums of science and philosophy – conundrums at which its orthodox practitioners foolishly insisted on tilting like champions – as a tired old hobo with holes in its shoes and its pockets turned inside-out. Just as physics must now yield once again to metaphysics, as it has done so many times before, so must the physicalistic abortion that currently passes for psychology.

The rehabilitation of psychology will be complete only when its partial physical interpretation has been extended to include the metaphysical ingredients of reality on which a meaningful definition of *mind* clearly depends ... in short, when it remembers its spiritual origins and takes its place as one of many integrated disciplines within the CTMU "master-language", SCSPL.

January 31, 2018

QUANTUM THEORY

QM and CTMU

184. What does Chris Langan think of quantum theory, and how does it relate to his Cognitive-Theoretic Model of the Universe (CTMU)?

Quantum theory is a quantum-probabilistic approximation of an overall theory of causation, the CTMU.

June 11, 2017

QUORA

Appealing

185. How do I appeal a Quora Moderation decision?

My advice would be not to bother, unless you have a lot of time to waste.
On at least two occasions when I tried to reasonably and politely defend myself from attacks against me and my ideas on this site, I was accosted

by Quora Moderation, which informed me that my supposed "violations" of "Be nice, be respectful!" policy had been summarily removed, but meanwhile allowed the initial attacks against me to stand despite the fact that there was nothing nice, respectful, or accurate about them. When I appealed, I was curtly informed – with no stated reason whatsoever – that the decision was final and would not change.

Despite the fact that this caused me to stop posting here, I'm still getting unwanted messages from these people, apparently due to belated squawking by my disgruntled detractors ... who, had they kept their unkind remarks to themselves in the first place, would have had nothing about which to run whining to the moderators.

I only know about my own situation, of course, and claim no knowledge of anyone else's. But for anyone in a situation like mine, this place is strictly no-win. If it starts looking the same from your own perspective, then perhaps a change of venue would be the easiest solution.

March 18, 2017

Debating

186. Why does Chris Langan disregard anyone who disagrees with him as intellectually inferior instead of addressing their argument and deconstructing it? Why is he always so skeptical of people being trolls, or have I misinterpreted their Quora activity?

Quora is not a debate club. I'm not paid to be here by Quora, and I don't have time to roll around on the floor wrestling with Quora trolls all day. (A Quora troll never admits it is wrong, cannot be educated, and only becomes more obnoxious when directly addressed by its target *du jour*.)

That being understood, I do not typically disregard coherent, meaningful arguments by informed, well-qualified, and well-vetted people who object to something in the CTMU. It's just that I never see any.

Rather than engage in debate with Quora trolls – an activity from which I have nothing whatsoever to gain – I've made a good deal of CTMU material freely available on the web.

Interested readers are invited to take full advantage of it.

August 17, 2018

Gould, John

187. What does John Gould think about CTMU?

Obviously, John Gould has done quite a lot of talking about the CTMU right here on Quora. One might be tempted to infer from this that he knows just about everything there is to know of it.

However, as the sole author of the CTMU, I can state with complete certainty that this is anything but the case. Despite the several attempts I've made to set Mr. Gould straight on various points of relevance, he continues to make precisely the same errors regarding it that he has made in the past. It's like being locked in an empty discotheque with the exits sealed, a skipping record on the platter, and the speakers cranked up to 150+ decibels.

I'm not trying to say that John Gould is an especially stupid person; that's not the case. He manages to say some relatively intelligent things on occasion. But that's what makes it all the more disappointing, and ultimately more irritating, when he makes glaring mistakes and then automatically defaults to "infinite loop" mode. It's like trying to sleep with a nuclear-powered cricket in the room.

What I'm saying is that Mr. Gould has an angry little bee in his bonnet regarding the CTMU, and that possibly due to a touch of OCD – we all have a little of that, by the way – he would probably be harder to detach from it than a five-pound lobster with one's fingers pinched between its claws.

So the long and short of it is simply this: John Gould is "attached" to the CTMU, and inasmuch as the attachment has nothing to do with an actual understanding of it, the attachment may contain a certain *emotional* element.

If only the emotion were of a positive and constructive nature.

September 28, 2018

Hostility

188. Why do comments which disagree with Chris Langan/CTMU keep disappearing from Quora?

Owing to the double whammy of being known for high intelligence and metaphysical (anti-physicalist) reasoning, I'm often stalked by pests. Or perhaps it's simply because I'm a little better-known out here in the real world than most Quora participants, and thus seem an attractive target for those who would take a shortcut to notoriety by forcing me to recognize their existence in order to siphon off a little public recognition.

Unfortunately, this army of pests includes several Quorans who have displayed a marked tendency to "specialize in my case". Not only have some of them posted misleading, prejudicial, impertinent, and sometimes downright toxic answers for questions about me and/or my work, especially the CTMU, but where permitted to do so, they've been observed to clog up the comments sections of my own answers with ad hominem nonsense which violates Quora's "be nice, be respectful" policy. In short, they are neither nice nor respectful.

Sometimes – but only in the worst cases – I delete their comments, thus saving Quora Moderation the necessity of removing them. I suggest that if one doesn't want one's comments removed, one *be nice and respectful*. (A bit of veracity wouldn't hurt either.)

[Note: I should also mention that I don't have time to play games here on Quora, especially games which have no entertainment value for me. Accordingly, I've deleted an exchange in the comments between "two" characters using what appear to be pictures of the same individual on "their" accounts, one of them vaguely resembling Jack Sparrow from "Pirates of the Caribbean" and the other merely foppish. No more of this nonsense, please.]

February 20, 2018

Trolling

189. What is Chris Langan up to these days?

Thank you for asking!

I'm running my 140 acre ranch. I'm seeing to Mega Foundation business. I'm working on the next round of CTMU material. And I've even found the time to answer a few questions here on Quora!

But speaking of which, I've also been forced to take up a new hobby: riding herd on a couple of tireless, utterly implacable, and often vicious little trolls who follow me around here like flapping, squeaking vampire bats with claws full of hungry, writhing leeches.

(One absurdly claims to have authored a "naturalistic" theory of "metaphysics" – roughly speaking, this is like going off one's meds, sticking one's snout high in the air, sliding one's hand under the lapel of one's smelly, brown-stained hospital gown, and imperiously proclaiming oneself to be Napoleon Bonaparte – while the other merely considers himself to be a victim of my alleged unceasing racial and cultural discrimination, crying out plaintively for justice.)

I keep hoping that I can dispense with the hobby.

February 24, 2018

190. Why does Chris Langan get so much praise on Quora?

Oh, please. The undeniable fact is that I attract far more trolling than praise on Quora. There are "Top Writers" here who have trolled me viciously in spiteful, misleading, profanity-laced tirades, received literally thousands of upvotes for doing so, and resisted all attempts to remove their defamation despite repeated complaints. Meanwhile, I get at most a few dozen upvotes for unique, informative, demonstrably correct answers that they couldn't have duplicated if they were given several centuries in which to do so, and have been subjected to the removal of dozens of my own well-reasoned comments defending myself and my work from troll attacks. If I were looking for "praise", this would be one of the last places in the world I'd come for it.

February 3, 2018

Veaux, Franklin

191. Is Franklin Veaux qualified to attack the CTMU by Chris M. Langan?

Absolutely not. Mr. Veaux has not only demonstrated what can only be called thorough incomprehension of the CTMU, but lacks the technical background that one would need in order to meaningfully criticize it or even comment intelligently on the field of metaphysics.

March 15, 2018

RATIONAL WIKI

Pseudointellectual trap

192. How does Rational Wiki compare to Less Wrong?

"Less Wrong" appears to be a Q&A site, perhaps a bit like Quora itself. As can be expected of such sites, it is slanted and not without its share of uninformed and/or objectionable opinion, but occasionally affords a modicum of useful information.

In contrast, "Rational Wiki" is a website which is designed to look like Wikipedia, but which is actually more like a pseudointellectual tourist trap whose inhabitants are fiercely dedicated to the mockery and defamation of people and ideas to which its proprietor objects. (As nearly as anyone can determine, this is an obscure Canadian resident and "secular humanist" calling himself "Trent Toulouse".) It exhibits a strong and persistent bias against conservatives, roundly insulting and belittling non-leftists at every available opportunity. It is also noted for its boundless contempt for religion and metaphysics, dismissing anything its contributors find difficult to understand as "nonsense" or "woo". Unlike Wikipedia, the site appears to have no clean-up crew(s) responsible for toning down the vitriol of its editorializers.

As I know from long personal experience, Mr. Toulouse and his gaggle of mostly pseudonymous partisans go after people and ideas they dislike quite aggressively. They've been going after me for years, always ranking high on the Google pages returned on my name. They've even taken to posting pictures of me with silly captions, doing their very best to make sure that none of their readers takes anything I say the least bit seriously. Such monkeyshines are unconstrained and apparently receive in-house encouragement.

Unfortunately, although these juvenile tactics fool no one with any intelligence, the misinformation shows no sign of abating, and its purveyors show no sign of even trying to comprehend the ideas they criticize. In the case of my own work, this means that they exhibit no understanding of metaphysical philosophy or the logic on which it properly comes to rest.

Browsers beware. With sites like this all over the place, a search engine can be a very dangerous thing. ;)

July 18, 2017

REALITY

Accepting syntax

193.   Do you agree with Chris Langan that all things share a common
       reality and are to that extent similar, and that the mere fact that
       two things can be discussed through the same syntax (e.g., the
       English language) shows their difference isn't absolute?

Yes, I'm Chris Langan, and I usually agree with myself. To that extent,
this answer belabors the obvious. But if I may, let me explain something
brand spanking new to those of you who have already answered this
question in such a way as to betray severe confusion about really hard
concepts like *reality, structure,* and *language.*

That thing you've been typing on, and at whose screen you've been staring
until your beady little eyes cross, is called a *computer,* and computation
theory is the branch of science which studies *what it does* ("compute").
You even do a little computation of your own, *mentally* speaking, and
according to many big experts who claim to know what they're talking
about, your body does likewise, *physically* speaking. So let's begin with
a little elementary computation theory, shall we?

If you were the kind of abstract automaton called an *acceptor* – which,
by the way, represents all kinds of actual concrete automata built on
its template, and even biological systems including you – you would
(*do,* in fact) have something called *accepting syntax.* Conformance to
this syntax – and by the way, "conforming to" means "sharing structure
with" – is the criterion which allows you to *accept* some things as input
while rejecting others.

For those of you capable of understanding it, this establishes that
you "share structure" with everything that you can accept as input,
i.e., *recognize* or *perceive.* What structure do I mean? Why, accepting
syntax, of course – that part of your programming and/or basic architec-
ture that controls what you accept as "real" and what you cannot. (Yes,
yes, I know – you're a big shot who can decide all by yourself what you
do or do not "accept as real". But there are others to consider, and the
replicability criterion of scientific observation implies that we all have
a standard accepting syntax controlling our perception. In fact, even

when you just imagine something, it is *recognizable* to you only because it superficially conforms to this syntax! But I digress.)

Now, are we all following along here? At this point, we should all understand that we have an accepting syntax, and that things we perceive must conform to it and in fact share structure with it.

Just to make sure that we all understand this, let's have a little pop quiz.

Doesn't this mean that whenever you see two things you regard as "different", both of them conform to (share structure with) accepting syntax, and therefore have something in common, namely, the generic structure of the aforementioned accepting syntax?

But doesn't this imply that all that you see, feel, touch, smell, and/or taste has a nonempty structural intersect?

But doesn't this mean that everything you can perceive is *the same* in this respect?

And doesn't that mean that it's *not totally different* from anything else you can see, feel, touch, smell, and/or taste ?

ANSWER KEY: **Yes, it does**.

Any questions? (If so, that's too bad, because at this point, still having questions would mean that you've got so many loose screws that if you stop clutching your head in consternation, it just might roll off your shoulders and bounce away like a tennis ball.)

We all know that abstraction can be hard ... for some, *very, very* hard. But let's get real here – if you're the kind of person who has trouble with this level of abstraction, then why are you trying to critique a theory that requires the highest level of abstraction possible?

I mean, shouldn't you be playing with matches in a haymow or something?

August 10, 2018

First causation

194. Why does Chris Langan state in the CTMU that the randomness of DNA mutations in Darwinian evolution is indeterminate and thus "magic" when there are clear deterministic explanations of how this randomness arises?

Because "random determinacy" is an oxymoron. Even statistical determinacy and mathematical chaos merely consist of microscopic events which themselves have no ultimate explanation, and therefore do not qualify as fully determinate. Full determination requires not just the full expression of a standard causal function including all parameters and inputs, but ordinal completion ("first causation" or causal closure). [In fact, it requires even more than that, but this should be enough to chew for now.]

February 10, 2018

Indispensability of logic

195. What is CTMU? Is it worth my time to understand it?

One cannot understand the reality that one inhabits without the CTMU. Therefore, if one wishes to understand reality, oneself, and one's embedment in reality, one should at least try to come to grips with it.

Perhaps this will be easier to understand if we put it another way. One should try to understand the CTMU for the same reason that one should study logic, only more so. The CTMU can be characterized as logic formulated on a very high level of discourse, and specifically as the level of metalogic which identifies logic itself as a central ingredient of intelligible reality.

On the other hand, if one is a Quora troll – especially the kind which always leads off by identifying itself as an atheist or a skeptic – then one needn't bother, as in this case, one lacks the intellectual acuity to make any headway.

August 10, 2018

Methodological inadequacies

196. What do mathematicians/physicists out there think about the Cognitive-Theoretic Model of the Universe article by Chris Langan (attached) that suggests that our current methods for understanding reality are fundamentally flawed?

As the author of the CTMU, let me state for the record that I don't recall saying that "current methods for understanding reality are fundamentally flawed." What I've been saying, more or less, is that *certain* methods of understanding reality are fundamentally *inadequate to explore reality in its metaphysical entirety*. These are different statements.

I can also state that no one who fails to acknowledge the shortcomings of certain methods of understanding reality is competent as a philosopher, and that such a person may be less than fully competent as a scientist or mathematician as well.

March 1, 2018

Self-communication

197. How would someone explain the CTMU (Cognitive-Theoretic Model of the Universe) to a child?

"When we talk to each other like we are right now, we're using something called a *language*. A language is something we use to communicate, just like you and I are doing when we talk to each other. It has symbols just like the letters on your alphabet blocks, words like *cat, dog,* and *skittles,* and sentences like 'See Spot run!', all of which help us tell each other what we mean.

"Well, every part of the world talks to itself and to other parts, and the CTMU is the language that it uses! Right now, I'm using the language called 'English' (French, German, Russian, Chinese,...) to talk to you and tell you what I mean. You can understand me because you understand English (etc.) the same way I do. When the world (cosmos, universe,...) talks to itself, it uses the CTMU!

"Remember, we say that a language is 'mathematical' because it's a bit like the counting numbers you use when you count to ten. Not only can you use those numbers to count; you can also use them to add, subtract, multiply, and divide (those are called 'operations'). You can even tell when one number is bigger or smaller than another (those are called 'relations')!

"Mathematical languages like the CTMU also have mathematical relations and operations just like the counting numbers. So we can always be exact, and the other person – if he or she is paying proper attention – can always understand what we mean. When the universe talks to itself using the CTMU, it always knows what it means as well!"

(Notice the part about "paying attention". Nature always pays attention to itself. Only the strange and unnatural phenomena calling themselves "philosophical naturalists" seem completely unable to do so with any success. ;)

March 15, 2018

198.   How can you explain CTMU to a layman?

Reality necessarily *communicates* (exchanges information) with itself; it sends information on states, events, and processes from place to place within itself by various means of transmission and induction. By definition, the medium of communication is *language*; that is, language can be generically defined as "the medium of information and communication". **It follows that reality has linguistic structure.**

Unfortunately for science, most scientific languages are structurally inadequate to perform linguistic functions like communication on reality's behalf.(1) However, the definition of language can be furnished with extra structure that overcomes these inadequacies. **The language defined to overcome these inadequacies, thus enabling the self-communication of reality, is called the CTMU.** (Note that this definition is functional, logico-mathematical, and independent of empirical induction and special terminology.)

Because the existence and validity of the CTMU (as just defined) are logical, ontological, and epistemological necessities, there is no escape from its implications. Laymen – and for that matter, amateur and professional scientists, mathematicians, philosophers, and theologians – have no chance of legitimately prevailing in arguments against it, and should avoid baseless complaints about its allegedly "unscientific" or "conjectural" nature.

[(1): For example, ordinary scientific languages are not self-contained; they have extrinsic requirements such as external processors, e.g., human minds or computers, to execute their operations. This prevents them from modeling their content, reality at large, well enough to generate and carry the information that reality needs in order to function. The CTMU, on the other hand, is ontologically self-contained with respect to all required objects, structures, and operations.]

May 28, 2018

Self-containment

199. (1) What exactly is Chris Langan trying to convey in the CTMU (in layman's terms), and (2) what is his goal/expectation in doing so?

(1) I'm trying to convey the deepest and most general formal characterization of the structure of reality. Specifically, I'm trying to convey the fact that reality as a whole takes the form of a certain uniquely structured and profoundly self-contained language.

(2) My goal is to help mankind avoid the nasty but at least partially avoidable pain and misery that it recurrently brings upon itself due to its substantial ignorance of the structure and meaning of the reality that it inhabits.

February 18, 2018

200. A key principle of the CTMU is that reality is self-contained. Can you really debunk this position and formulate the alternative?

The self-containment of reality cannot be debunked. It's a logical necessity.

Even a drunken monkey could see it: if there were anything *outside reality* on which reality were in any way dependent (for origination, causation, support, maintenance, or anything else), then the entire dependency relationship would be *real* and therefore *inside reality*. Therefore, reality is self-contained with respect to physical and metaphysical functions like origination, causation, support, maintenance, etc. (QED).

This is what logicians call a *proof by contradiction*, and it invalidates the premise of external relevance. (Sorry, but there's simply nothing else to give way here.) It also means that the level of reality we're talking about is the deepest level possible ... the CTMU level. That's because "reality is self-contained" doubles as a *definition* of reality which makes it idempotent under inclusion (or if one likes, "self-inclusive", with all the bells and whistles required to make it work). The CTMU develops the implications of this and certain other facts from first principles.

One really needs to understand how logic works on the metaphysical level of discourse to reason properly about metaphysical questions like the origin of reality, "dark energy", and so on. On the other hand, if you're trying to explain things on a more superficial level, then your explanation is incomplete, and once again, you don't get to take credit for anything I've already figured out.

I thoroughly understood the tautological implications of self-containment thirty years ago, which is about how long the CTMU has been around. I hope no one thinks he's going to get over on me now.

July 11, 2018

Self-reference

201. Are Russell's Paradox, Godel's Incompleteness Theorem, and the Halting Problem just different instantiations of the same underlying difficulty? (If not, what are interesting differences?)

The "underlying difficulty" you evidently mean is called "self-reference" in a formal context and "self-inclusion" in set theory. These concepts are not themselves inconsistent, but seem problematical because they permit the formulation of paradoxes ("this sentence is false", "this theorem is unprovable") and/or apparently inconsistent mathematical constructions (the set of all sets, Russell's set of all non-self-inclusive sets).

At one time, various formalisms were "immunized" against such constructions by simply forbidding self-reference across the board, or by changing the names of things so that they couldn't display it (basically: "If X looks like it might self-refer / self-include, reclassify it or change its name so that it can't!"). But this was entirely uncalled-for and misleading, as reality itself is self-referential in the sense that it has various reflexive properties and incorporates various operations which act on it and functions that "take it as an argument". Given that reality makes extensive use of self-reference, no scientific or mathematical case can be made against it.

The self-referential nature of reality has been thoroughly developed in a theory called the CTMU, around which various supposedly intelligent people have been completely unable to wrap their heads. Of course, most of them swear that it's not them, but the theory. However, their stupefaction at best reflects an unfortunate glitch in their own thought processes. Just as in Turing's solution of Hilbert's *Entscheidungsproblem*, their minds exhibit a tendency to spiral into infinite loops at any mention of certain "forbidden" ideas.

In any case, self-reference is something that no conscious human being can avoid, as it constitutes the essence of self-awareness.

October 8, 2017

Syntactic metaverse

202. Are there meta-simultaneous universes within reality, according to the CTMU theory of Chris Langan? How are they related to our world?

In the CTMU, alternate universes exist in syntax as semantic potential. (This does not equate to the full concrete existence ascribed to them by other theories; it is not automatically guaranteed that a given potential reality is anywhere realized.)

May 12, 2018

True structure

203. What can the simple man or woman expect from Christopher Langan's Cognitive-Theoretic Model of the Universe (CTMU)?

The CTMU affords a basic understanding of God, Man, the human soul (which connects God and Man), and the true metalogical structure of reality. All that its comprehension requires is moderate intelligence, basic literacy, an open mind, and an honest effort to understand a well-structured metaphysical alternative to the current naturalistic (physicalistic, materialistic, "secular") paradigm.

Regardless of the excuses thus far offered by the confused and disgruntled for their incomprehension – very few of which repose any blame whatsoever on those who concoct them – it is the conceptual inertia of the naturalistic paradigm, plus certain mostly negative emotions and biases, that presently stand in the way.

Let's hope that it is still possible to change this for the better.

January 9, 2018

Ultimate Reality

204. What is the ultimate reality?

Ultimate reality is described by a unique metaphysical formulation of logic called the *Cognitive Theoretic Model of the Universe* (CTMU). This description is not a product of guesswork, but is as real and verifiable as it can possibly be. No other description is even remotely viable; any description which fails to conform to the CTMU is logically precluded.

February 13, 2018

205. What does "ultimate reality" mean to you?

"Ultimate reality" is the level of reality that is both comprehensive and irreducible to anything deeper or more fundamental. (There are many technical properties that go along with these criteria, but this is the gist of it.)

May 21, 2018

206. Can we ever know the ultimate reality?

Of course we can, at least to an extent.

Because ultimate reality is induced from reality as we know it as a terminal generalization thereof, it couples with reality as we know it, and can thus be known through the coupling (in particular, it must have structural properties which make it amenable to inductive coupling; *amenability to inductive coupling* is itself a logical property, and all necessary supporting properties are thereby implied). Conversely, if "ultimate reality" *cannot* be known in any way through the inductive coupling, then it does not couple logically with reality as we know it, and cannot be meaningfully called "reality" at all.

The unique metaphysical formulation of logic which elucidates the structure of ultimate reality, otherwise known as "God", is called the *Cognitive Theoretic Model of the Universe* (CTMU). The CTMU is a true "theory of everything" in the logical sense, i.e., the only sense in which a true theory of everything can actually exist.

February 13, 2018

REALITY PRINCIPLE

Valid tautology

207. Do you agree with Chris Langan that reality contains all that is real and only that which is real, and that if there was anything real enough to in any way influence reality, it would have to be inside reality?

I'm afraid that there's no way to disagree. This has been correctly identified as a tautology, albeit *misidentified* as a mere *propositional* tautology which cannot be refined to obtain useful information.

I'm not quite sure where those who deny this assertion learned what they persist in calling "logic", but one thing is for sure: they need to get their money back. ;)

August 16, 2018

RECYCLING

Logical fallacies

208. What is an example of logical fallacy about recycling?

The main recycling fallacy is the assumption that things are directly "recycled", i.e. put to the same specific uses to which they were originally put in the form they originally took. This is not generally the case. In fact, they must usually be reduced to some prior form from which new products serving new purposes can be made in different sizes and shapes.

This is sometimes an extremely expensive process, and sometimes it leads to more pollution than the recycled materials themselves. It is typically claimed that "science will find a way". Unfortunately, this claim usually turns out to be a way for certain privileged parties to stuff their pockets, much in the way that "closing the nuclear fuel cycle" was nothing but a toxic flatus in the breeze intended to narcotize the public as certain unscrupulous parties did their business in the field of nuclear energy ... i.e., stuffed their pockets. (Big surprise, right?)

And let's not forget our wonderful political hacks, who make careers out of inflating pseudoscientific pipe dreams into gilt-edged "done deals". Yes, there's no easier route to political success than promising technological fixes for urgent problems while squandering every tax dime squeezed out of the "little people" on the military-industrial-security complex-cum-burgeoning welfare state. Come one, come all!

That being said, recycling isn't always a bad idea. But never buy a jalopy without kicking the tires and poking around under the hood.

October 6, 2017

RELIGION

Interpreting religions

209. What religions are not compatible with Christopher Langan's
Cognitive-Theoretic Model of the Universe (CTMU)?

All logically consistent religions are compatible with the CTMU in the
sense that they can be interpreted (or modeled) within it. This follows
from the fact that the CTMU is a metaphysical extension of logic in
which logic can metalogically refer to itself.

January 26, 2018

SCIENCE

Methodological inadequacies

210.   Why do so many scientists (and other "educated" people) accept
        the "Big Bang" theory when it contradicts one of the fundamen-
        tal axioms of all knowledge: cause and effect?

First, most scientists are not extensively trained to properly evaluate
the logical integrity of scientific theories; surprisingly, this is not typically an ingredient of scientific curricula. By the nature of their training,
scientists are often quite effective in working out the mathematical
details of their fields, but the big picture sometimes escapes them without necessarily interfering with the solution of the specific problems in
which they are interested.

Secondly, while there exists a valid causal framework which accommo-
dates the Standard Model, most scientists are totally unfamiliar with it.

April 16, 2018

Problem of induction

211. Why do physicists ignore the problem of induction? Do they assume it has a solution?

They ignore it because they lack the kind of knowledge that would enable them to sort it out. The simple fact is that the problem of induction precludes certainty for theories derived exclusively by empirical induction and confirmed by observation, and this qualifies as a very inconvenient truth for not just physicists but the entire "hard science" community.

In my personal experience, not only are most physicists unequipped to deal with such irreducibly epistemological and therefore metaphysical problems; they are hostile to those who can. If there's one thing that typical academic physicists love to do, it is to disparage philosophy in general as extraneous gobbledygook, thus excusing themselves from having to pay attention to anyone but other physicists. It's the case-hardened lock on the clubhouse door.

On a very high level of reasoning, the problem of induction can be (and has been) solved. The solution is called the *CTMU*, short for *Cognitive Theoretic Model of the Universe*. But while this solution is logically all but immune to criticism, no one should hold one's breath waiting for physicists – almost all of whom consider themselves natural philosophers *par excellence* – to come to grips with it.

Nothing against physicists, mind you. Some of them are downright brilliant. But they really need to stick to physics, and leave metaphysical thinking to those specifically equipped for it.

June 7, 2018

Proving God

212. Why do scientists remind us that there is no proof of God when the arguments for Big Bang or Evolution are only based on evidence and testability?

Because of wishful thinking. No scientist has any way whatsoever of knowing that "there is no proof of God"; it just so happens that many of them have been told this all their lives by people whom they (mistakenly) considered to be experts on the subject, and many others simply like the idea of ruling it out. In any case, if there were a proof that no proof of God's existence is possible, it would not utilize the scientific method; it would necessarily be logico-mathematical in character. Such reasoning is better left to mathematical logicians with considerable knowledge of philosophy and theology.

May 2, 2017

Scientific method

213. What is Chris Langan's analysis of the scientific method?

The Scientific Method, which is central to the traditional methodology of the empirical sciences, is a dualistic metalanguage which purports to govern the bidirectional mapping between theory and observation. It is dualistic in the sense that theory is made entirely dependent on empirical observation, with absolutely no dependency in the opposite direction aside from the choice of which experiments to run and which observations to make.

The Scientific Method can be helpful in shaping constructive feedback between theory and experimentation, but obviously breaks down at the level of scientific inquiry on which observed reality cannot be properly described by dualism (because absolute dualism precludes observation itself).

Reality is ultimately monic, as otherwise it would be disconnected and therefore two or more realities instead of one. Because these separate realities would be incommunicado (being cut off from each other by absolute dualism), they could not interact at all, and the inhabitants of one could not recognize another.

Addendum (originally in response to a troll who evidently had my response to his own comment deleted, and whose comment was therefore deleted in turn):

If theorization and observation were not coupled in a very specific way by the Scientific Method, one could simply dispense with it. In that case, no one would ever have made a big deal out of it. Instead, students would simply be told "Get to making observations and theorizing about them!"

But it's not as simple as that. The observations have to be selected in such a way that the associated observation statements confirm or falsify the theory – this often involves the careful design and execution of experiments – and the theory has to be developed in a way that explains existing observations and/or predicts others.

This coordination of theorization and observation is what the Scientific Method is all about. This is how it "mediates" between them.

July 8, 2018

Standard model vs CTMU

214. If scientists can't really explain what the state of the universe was in before the 'big bang' and how it came to be that way, why is it taken seriously?

As an answer has been requested of me, and as this question keeps showing up in my feed, I'll answer it. (This is not to be construed as an invitation to attack.)

The Standard Model is taken seriously because, as a partial model of physical causation which omits origination and falls short of complete determinacy, it works pretty well. That is, it is often (but not always) confirmed by prediction and experimentation.

The Standard Model comprises a theoretical language that is often generically referred to as "physics". However, in order to discuss the origin or "initial state" of reality, a higher-order "metaphysical" language is required ... a language in which the physical aspect of cosmic evolution can be analyzed and justified.

In the 1980's, I provided such a language. It's called the "CTMU", standing for the "Cognitive Theoretic Model of the Universe". It can be described as a reflexive metaphysical metalanguage of the object-language "physics" and its observational universe of discourse.

In the CTMU, the physical aspect of reality occupies a certain limit. The nature of this limit has been described in several academic publications (although one would never know it by the troll attacks to which it has recurrently been subject due to its theological implications).

As the CTMU is supertautological – because it has a structure which amounts to a global, self-contained analogue of propositional tautology – it has a certain metalogical property which can best be described as "logical self-veracity".

It is therefore extremely safe to say that this is where metaphysical extensions of standard physics are headed, whether or not any particular physicist or philosopher happens to like it.

January 22, 2018

SIMULATION THEORY

Self-simulation

215. Within the context of Christopher Langan's Cognitive-Theoretic Model of the Universe (CTMU), could we technically be in a computer simulation of sorts, with 'God' being the programmer?

Yes. According to the CTMU, reality can be understood as a "self-simulation", at least in the sense that what we see outside of ourselves – the physical universe – conceals the process which actually produces it, and cannot account for the entirety of what producing it actually requires.

However, the simulation is not merely computational in the mechanical sense, but (in CTMU terminology) "protocomputational" or "precomputational". That is, it utilizes a kind of "metaprocessing" called *telic recursion*, which generates **entire timelines** instead of individual events.

God is indeed the Programmer-in-Chief, but does His "programming" largely through secondary sensor-controllers, including human beings, which locally inhabit the simulation. As for God Himself, He distributes over the entire simulation and is therefore omnipresent.

The entire simulation can be reduced to a master "programming language" sometimes referred to as *Logos*, which is *trialic*, serving as its own universe and model. On a more technical level, it is known as the CTMU.

January 31, 2018

216. Are there any theoretical universal models that are not causal by nature? For instance, if this was a simulation as suggested, then how might the rules be different?

Yes. The definitive theory is called the CTMU, short for *Cognitive Theoretic Model of the Universe*. Publications date from the late 1980's through the present, most recently in the peer-reviewed academic journal *Cosmos and History*. Technically, it is a theory of mathematical metaphysics.

Basically, the CTMU says that reality is an ontologically closed "self-simulation" in the precise sense that it contains empirically undecidable "programming" as well as "displayed" observational content, and that its logico-mathematical structure is that of a self-structuring, self-axioma- tizing "SCSPL", short for *Self-Configuring Self-Processing Language*. This language has a unique form called a *supertautology,* according to which its evolution is *metacausal* rather than strictly causal.

In addition, the CTMU embodies a logical form of self-similarity anal- ogous to the so-called "holographic principle" as later developed in connection with string theory. Accordingly, it is *trialic*, effecting a distributive coincidence of theory, universe, and model in a coherent "metaformal system".

Last but not least, the CTMU was authored by a man reputed, at least in some circles, to be the most intelligent in the world.

April 26, 2018

217. What is Chris Langan's view on the simulation hypothesis?

The CTMU is the first and only viable ontological theory of reality as a self-simulation. I wrote the CTMU. Hence, I have a high opinion of it.

June 23, 2018

218. Is the CTMU the first simulation theory?

Yes, the CTMU is the first detailed theory of reality as a self-simulation, having been used to resolve Newcomb's Paradox in 1989. (Note that real- ity must be a *"self*-simulation" insofar as that which does the simulating must itself be real.)

This in itself was a milestone; it seems to have been the first time that a major philosophical problem was solved in the context of a computa- tionally simulated reality. While it had previously been suggested that our world is somehow embedded in a wider insensible reality – e.g., Plato's Allegory of the Cave – this was the first time that an existing philosophical problem was solved in an explicitly computational setting.

Note that the CTMU has a unique theoretic structure that is absolutely necessary for this purpose, and that its functionality exceeds that of ordinary computers (it was, and is, described as "protocomputational"). No other so-called "simulation theory" shares this property, ostensibly because the authors of such theories fail to understand the deep structure of reality and the limitations of standard automata.

September 14, 2018

SOCIAL MEDIA

Stratified hive

219. What did you assume was exaggerated until you experienced it?

Counterfactual groupthink and Kafkaesque bureaucratic skullduggery within social media / online social networks.

One tends to assume that such networks are all about the communication and dissemination of real, valid information for the good of society and the people comprising it, and sometimes this is actually the way it works. But each network has a business model and a tiny handful of self-interested people riding it, and deviating from their POV nearly always results in censorship and other abuses. Being the champion of certain unpopular truths (which I have an established ability to cram down the throat of any opponent in fair debate, so to speak), I'm in a special position to know this. Every time I see myself and my ideas being run down by opinionated ignoramuses in this or that social medium, I show up to defend them ... only to have it once more brought to my attention that almost no one is on the side of truth these days.

I've generally tried to find the best I could in people, and this is how I initially approached social media. I heard people complaining about how they're often run autocratically, even whimsically or perversely, but I'd ask myself: given the First Amendment of the US Constitution, how bad could it possibly be? Unfortunately, it turns out that the answer is "pretty bad indeed". I recently had a good deal of truthful and potentially valuable dialogue erased by the moderators of one of these fora, apparently in order to protect a longstanding contributor who had initially attacked me, but was trying to cover his tracks after finding himself on the losing end of an exchange with me. He whined to the moderators, and I suddenly became the "aggressor". Just another bad show in an ever-longer run of them.

The Internet Hive Mind is defined as an entity consisting of numerous individuals whose exchange of knowledge and opinions leads ideally to emergent collective intelligence, but can also lead to deadening conformity. We have on the one hand a potential for group intelligence to emerge from a distributed, self-organizing "human computation" occurring on a given proprietary software platform, and on the other, the actual reality of hives in nature and the human economy: they naturally stratify into classes, one of which runs the show and the other of which provides myriad group-thinking drones and workers for the pleasure of those in the steering compartment. Where monopoly capitalism ices the socialist cake, the freedom of people to spontaneously come together to achieve a truthful consensus is nonviable. Instead, social media implicitly provide an ideologically constrained setting in which the most exigent contributors, having slavishly "gotten with the program" of those higher up in the hive, sneakily pull strings and push levers to game forum policies and manipulate bureaucratic processes to their advantage. The result generally has nothing whatsoever to do with truth.

Participants need to question who is running the hives to which they belong, and what they're actually about. Just because you haven't yet found yourself on the wrong side of the ideology prevailing in a given forum doesn't mean that you won't, should you ever appreciably deviate from it. Have a look around you. Are the proprietors avowed atheists? Religious fanatics? Singularity-preaching techie plutocrats? Do they prefer globalism to national sovereignty and local democratic self-determination? Is there a strange alignment of contributor opinion with the publicly stated views and narratives of the proprietors? Are there any improbable confluences of opinion that appear to have been engineered?

Needless to say, this trend is not pointed in the best direction for launching and propelling humankind into the New Millennium. But for the time being, on the increasingly slim chance of opening a few minds and doing a little good, I'll remain open to limited participation.

May 2, 2017

SOCIETY

Sustainability

220. How does a global society behave that finally comes to accept that Christopher Langan's Cognitive-Theoretic Model of the Universe (CTMU) is true?

This question can be rephrased as follows:

How does a society behave that accepts truth on the physical and metaphysical levels?

It behaves more sustainably and with greater resilience than a society anchored to a flawed, inexorably sinking worldview. It offers real meaning to its members, and is not disrupted by frequent descents into irrationality. And by encouraging intellectual competence and creativity, it has the potential to maintain a high general standard of living.

February 19, 2018

SUPERTAUTOLOGY

Absolutization of truth

221. Is the CTMU absolute truth? If so, why?

Yes, the CTMU is absolute truth in a sense roughly analogous to that in which a propositional tautology is absolute truth, but in the expanded context of a new metaformal linguistic construct called a *supertautology*. (This has been defined and explained at length in several peer-reviewed papers – don't be afraid to do a little homework.)

Just as a propositional tautology like "X or not-X" is true regardless of the truth values of its sentential variables, the CTMU supertautology is true regardless of the form taken by specific scientific theories therein, and can thus guide the formulation of scientific theories in general. Metalogically, it amounts to an advanced reflexive formulation of model theory which utilizes brand new mathematics in explaining the "absolute" (self-verifying) nature of logic with respect to reality at large on the basis of direct intelligibility.

Because logic is the structure of truth, the absolutization of logic as a requirement of intelligibility amounts to the absolutization of truth. Thanks to a property known as "logical idempotence", the supertautology spans arbitrary levels of verification all the way up to metaphysical ontology. It is thus applicable in every scientific, mathematical, and philosophical domain.

Addendum: A reader asks the following question:

Question: Given Wittgenstein's statement that tautologies tell you nothing relevant about reality, why do tautologies take absolute precedence in your theory, and why is it so important that they be used in this way?

Answer: Before one can formulate a meaningful question about the CTMU, one must take the trouble to understand what it says ... for example, by reading the above response, which states that the CTMU is not a mere tautology, but a **supertautology**.

Whereas a tautology is just a circular expression within a language, a supertautology is an entire language configured in a tautological or circular way. In order to take on this structure, a language must assume certain unique and interesting properties. It is from this structure and these properties, which must be shared by the content of the language as a condition of its intelligibility therein, that interesting conclusions can be drawn regarding the content.

The CTMU leaves Wittgenstein and every philosopher before or since in the dust. But before one can understand how and why, one must make an effort to understand what the CTMU says about its own structure and its own properties. Again, **do your homework**. I've made study materials freely available, so it's no one's fault but yours if you fail to use them.

[**Warning**: Because the CTMU has theological ramifications unbeloved of "the atheist community" (if such we may call it), it has many implacable enemies on this site, not one of whom has ever displayed the slightest understanding of it. It is strongly suggested that readers not allow these trolls to mislead them.

A common ploy of such trolls is to demand a "prediction" of the CTMU. Some of these are history; e.g., an early one was that of accelerating cosmic expansion, for which the CTMU explanation has never been duplicated. But the short answer is that the CTMU does not rely on prediction; it relies on the fact that it provides necessary infrastructure for science in general.

A few less stupid (but still intellectually challenged) trolls have responded that science needs no infrastructure, as science already exists and it already works. However, it certainly *does* need infrastructure, and it certainly *does not* work on all levels – it tops out well beneath the metaphysical level of discourse occupied by extremely important questions regarding (e.g.) the ultimate nature and origination of reality, including quantum cosmology – and no scientist can explain why not. Hence, the CTMU is an absolute requisite of science.]

Note: Another answer has been posted to this question by a frequent (and just as frequently misinformed) CTMU critic, who states that "a tautology is a tautology with respect to a class of models." Quite so. To be more specific, a propositional tautology is absolutely true with respect to all *intelligible* models. We can forget about models outside of this class – after all, they are *unintelligible*, which means that you couldn't describe one of them even if you tried.

September 28, 2018

Logical core of metaphysics

222. Why is there a spate of Anonymous questions about the fringe CTMU conjecture?

As the sole author of the CTMU, I can only say that *if* this were true, I don't know why it *would* be. However, I can state with absolute certainty that whether or not the CTMU is "fringe", it is not a mere "conjecture". It's a supertautology, and one cannot worm one's way out of it. It's the everlasting adamantine logical core of mathematical metaphysics, and if one doesn't like it, one really needs to go out and find oneself another field, the actual state of which is more to one's liking (not that one can extricate oneself from its domain in any event).

[**Note**: This may be a troll question. In any case, my answer was requested by someone who uses the approving phrase "a fair analysis" to describe another (defamatory, collapsed) answer which alleges that I'm "irresponsible ... [with] a complete lack of moral conscience ... a pseudointellectual ... and sorry excuse for a genius". One can't explicitly endorse this kind of defamatory ad hominem tripe and not be considered as much a troll as the one who wrote it.]

March 1, 2018

Logical structure

223. How often does a theologist read an evidence-based argument against theism?

Never. (There aren't any, aside from one which atheists are intellectually incapable of comprehending.)

Evidence for a statement or theory X is generally applicable (instantiates X) only within the scope of any axioms or principles incorporated by X or implicit in the underlying model of X. However, the scope of X cannot usually be established within X itself, unless X has a very special structure.

This structure has been described on Quora as that of the CTMU Supertautology. This is the only context in which the meaningful probative power of evidence is unlimited, making it useful in deciding ontological issues like the existence of God. In this context, the existence of God is absolutely inescapable.

October 18, 2017

New mathematical system

224. Why does Chris Langan use the term "super-tautology"?

Isn't is obvious? "Supertautology" is a new and very important mathematical concept to which everyone had best get accustomed if one wants to understand the first thing about the true nature of reality. To reject supertautology is to reject the reality that we inhabit.

January 12, 2018

225. Is the CTMU true?

Yes, absolutely. Its structure is that of a *supertautology*, a new mathematical system which incorporates logic as a whole and thus ensures its own veracity.

[**Warning**: This site teems with anti-CTMU trolls and their sockpuppets, and the Quora moderation staff is completely inadequate to deal with them. Not one of these trolls has ever displayed any understanding whatsoever of the theory or any of its components. Answers to CTMU-related questions which do not come from me, or from someone whose statements can be checked against CTMU material published elsewhere, should be regarded as unreliable, especially if they are both pejorative and free of actual CTMU content. Thanks for your attention.]

September 30, 2018

SYNDIFFEONESIS

Common syntax requirement

226. What does concept of "syndiffeonesis" mean in Christopher Langan's Cognitive-Theoretic Model of the Universe (CTMU)?

Syndiffeonesis translates to "difference in sameness". It defines the generic relational structure of reality in terms of syntactic distribution and coherence: given any relationship of any arity and order, its synetic (invariant syntactic) level must distribute over its diffeonic (variable) level, which consists of things to be discerned or distinguished, thereby providing them with a unified basis of cognitive and/or perceptual coherence. Basically, it says that common (uniformly distributed) syntax is required in order for any number of things to be recognized, no matter how generically, as different or distinct, or to identify any one thing as different from its complement.

February 9, 2018

TEACHING

Social engineering

227. What controversial advice have people given to their children?

"Trust your teachers. They want what's best for you."

Modern teachers, bless their hearts, are in the indoctrination-and-socialization business. These days, trusting them blindly amounts to swallowing the social engineering imperatives of the socioeconomic elite, who want a 2-tier society consisting of a hereditary upper class which embraces global supercapitalistic corporate fascism in partnership with host governments, and a culturally and racially homogenized ("multicultural") lower class which stays on the ground, mewling pathetically with their mouths open for any crumbs that happen to fall off the upper-class table.

This might not be totally unjustifiable if there were a real standard of merit involved in class stratification, or for that matter in the education system. But unfortunately, one can only strain one's eyes and credulity trying to find it.

May 12, 2017

TELEOLOGY

Embracing truth

228. Does donating to Mega Foundation increase one's teleological value?

Well, that's rather a strange question, isn't it. (I wonder if it's sincere.)

Obviously, positive teleological value is not contingent on having money to donate to charitable causes – poor people can have it too. However, it is also true that a person who supports teleology by embracing and supporting truth to the best of his or her ability usually has greater teleological value that one who ignores it, rejects it, or opposes it.

Unfortunately, as we all know, most people with appreciable money and power couldn't give a hoot less about anything but their own future prospects, the rest of the population be damned. They wax philanthropical only when it wins them an instant pat on the head by the media and/or other rich and powerful people, improving their public image in such a way as to fatten their own bottom lines.

For the record, the Mega Foundation does not pander to such people.

February 19, 2018

Metaphysical optimization

229. Does Christopher Langan's Cognitive-Theoretic Model of the Universe do away with Hume's principle that one cannot derive an "ought" from an "is"?

Of course. "No ought from is" (Hume's Law, Hume's Guillotine) was just Hume's self-contradictory and therefore doomed attempt to turn his exclusion of *a priori* metaphysics into metaphysical preclusion.

Whereas Hume's bare-bones conceptualization of reality had no room for a metaphysical domain over which *that which is* can (and must) in some sense be optimized (*should* inevitably refers to such an optimization), the CTMU is explicitly metaphysical and therefore does not share this limitation.

Out of respect for standard philosophical terminology, the aspect of reality which makes *should* out of *is* (and vice versa) continues to go by the name **teleology**.

February 18, 2018

Self-reinforcing conatus

230. Chris Langan (author of CTMU) claims that he's logically proved atheists go to hell. To clarify, do atheists stay in hell for eternity, or only until they stop rejecting the possibility of God?

I don't recall publishing a proof that atheists go to hell (whether I can is another matter). If you can direct me to the exact statement to which you refer, perhaps I could comment at slightly greater length.

Meanwhile, remember that hell is necessary for not only the efforts of the Christian Church to curb attrition, but the welfare of society and mankind. For example, once an ambitious sociopath becomes a serial killer, mass murderer, hanging judge, bloodthirsty warlord, tyrannical emperor, evil dictator, crazed oligarch, rapacious international banker, or atheist-materialist techie billionaire who, by stealth or manipulation, can abuse other people with legal impunity (as nearly all successful sociopaths eventually do), society and mankind need a higher form of deterrence to protect them, and this is the very important function of hell.

As for whether hell is "real", that's a matter of valid metaphysical reasoning. This reasoning has much to do with a concept historically referred to as *teleology*, a self-reinforcing conatus by and for which the universe must include all necessary deterrents and safeguards, and the mathematical structure of metaphysical reality at large. Also important are the concepts of *God, free will,* and the *human soul*, on all of which I've previously commented on this site.

(Yes, hell is in some sense "real". But of course, this says nothing about the exact form that it will take for a given unregenerate miscreant. ;)

[**Addendum**: To those who insist on making an issue of my logic, please at least make an effort to understand it. First, hell is not a linear extension of the axes of spacetime, but is contained in an orthogonal expansion of spacetime; thus, objections based on the fact that "the dead no longer exist in space and time" are invalid. Secondly, one is not sent to hell for honest doubt or agnosticism, but for active denial or antitheism, i.e., blasphemy (among other things). This really doesn't require any proof, as it is a matter of common sense – one cannot survive in a metaphysical medium that one actively rejects and has encouraged others to actively reject. Instead, one is sent "in the opposite direction", so to speak ... to a complementary degenerative medium where identity is destroyed rather than sustained, refined, or transformed.

Many atheists seem to think that upon death, their minds will dissolve painlessly or perhaps even ecstatically into blackness or white light as though they were *arhats* or *bodhisattvas*, or perhaps just Kiefer Sutherland in "Lost Boys". But sadly for those of this optimistic persuasion, existence and identity aren't quite as easy to surrender as they might imagine. In fact, the utter dissolution of identity can be a process that is full of unimaginable pain and despair and which seems to last forever (or "for eternity", as religious people like to say.)

From here out it gets a bit more technical, but this should at least help put you on the right track regarding something that could – i.e., *will definitely* – end up being very important to you. A word to the wise.]

March 24, 2018

TELESIS

Ultimate reduction

231. What is the definition of "telesis" by Chris Langan in simple and sophisticated terms?

Telesis is the convergent generalization and ultimate reduction (product) of reality. Energy may be considered a limiting form of it. (If you don't understand what any of these words mean, please get a dictionary. You might also try reading a little something I've written.)

January 10, 2018

TELIC RECURSION

Metacausation

232. What does Telic Recursion mean in Christopher Langan's Cognitive-Theoretic Model of the Universe?

In the CTMU, telic recursion is "metacausation". That is, it is a level of the causal evolution of reality which distributes over standard causation and is orthogonal to it in the sense that it generates entire timelines (cause-effect event sequences, networks of quantum entanglement) as opposed to mere single events.

February 10, 2018

TELOR

Self-dual operator

233. What is the definition of "telor" by Chris Langan?

In the CTMU, a telor is self-dual operator which binds telesis. Human beings are telors. (Quora is not the proper venue for a full technical description at this time, as the typical Quora participant lacks the background necessary to understand it.)

January 12, 2018

THEORIZING

Theoretical principle

234. What is the meaning of a theoretical principle?

Let a theory or "theoretical language" **T** be defined as a set of strings {s*} of symbols s from the signature or "alphabet" S of **T**. (This is just the ordinary definition of "language" for certain general purposes, but with the label *theory* attached to make it a "*theoretical* language"; at its most general, a theory need be neither axiomatic nor even descriptive).

A theoretical principle P of **T** is just an expression of **T** (i.e., a member of the set of strings {s*} comprising **T**) to which an assignment of "importance" justifies the exalted title of "principle".

Whether P be an axiom, a definition, a heuristic, a piece of guesswork, or just an uninterpreted string, it has no meaning until it is interpretatively mapped into or onto a *universe* U in which meaning can be ascribed to it. Once this has been accomplished, we can then worry about providing the "importance" of P with a justification. E.g., we can require that P be especially useful or "instrumental" in U, or that P be true in *all* models (valid interpretations) of **T** in U, or that certain other expressions (well-formed strings of **T**) be derivable from P by substitution under the operative rules of deductive inference, or that P be an encapsulation of **T** into which a significant part of U and/or **T** itself can be inductively mapped, and so on.

In other words, the **meaning** of anything, including a principle of a theory **T**, resides in its **correspondence** to something, even if this is just the thing itself. Given this meaning, we can then decide whether it is sufficiently important to merit recognition as a "principle".

February 23, 2018

Theory of everything

235. Has Chris Langan published any other theory/theories other than the CTMU?

I define the CTMU as a true "theory of everything". So by definition, the CTMU absorbs all of my valid theoretical content.

(I seldom publish theoretical speculations, preferring to make sure that my ideas can be modeled in the CTMU before releasing them.)

February 9, 2018

TRIALITY

Cosmic self-containment

236. Can anyone give a quick summary of Christopher Langan's Cognitive-Theoretic Model of the Universe (CTMU)?

It couldn't possibly be simpler. The CTMU is a theory that is not *just* a theory, but also its own universe AND its own model therein. In other words, it is *trialic*. Triality is an implication of a mathematical property called *closure*, which is analogous to cosmic self-containment. Any so-called "Theory of Everything" (ToE) must exhibit this property. Among all of the ToE candidates out there, only the CTMU actually does so. There is only one way to construct a theory of this kind: as a *super-tautology*. A supertautology is simply the model-theoretic analogue of a propositional tautology, i.e., a tautology with ontological force. The entirety of modern empirical and mathematical science can be seamlessly embedded in this structure as a kind of limit.

Because of what it does, the CTMU may well be the single most important work of philosophy, theology, science, and mathematics ever conceived. Inasmuch as we will ever be privileged to truly know reality, we must know it as specified by this theory. When it comes to epistemology, the CTMU has no meaningful competition. In over thirty years, no one – regardless of claimed academic credentials and affiliations – has been able to put a dent of any kind in it, and due to its supertautological formulation, no one ever will.

This gives rise to a very important question: How is it possible for something like the CTMU to be discovered by a person who is subsequently introduced on every major television network in North America (and many abroad) as the "smartest man in America / the world", and still draw no attention from Academia? The answer is simple but profoundly disturbing: Academia, and the wider economy which unwisely relies on it, *also* exhibits self-containment and the associated mathematical closure property. Its constant accumulation of power and influence has now given it a virtual monopoly on scientific communication, intellectual commerce, and even the right to obtain a decent job on the basis of personal merit and intelligence.

Because Academia is closed, outsiders – people who have not paid tens or hundreds of thousands of dollars for its increasingly watered-down credentials – have no access to it, its personnel, or its journals. This allows it to exclude anything for which its own members cannot take exclusive credit (in any other context, this would amount to a "conspiracy to commit theft of intellectual property"). In my own case, there was never any choice about whether or not to obtain academic credentials, as not only did I lack the money to obtain them, but by some combination of error and contrivance which it is either unable or unwilling to explain, Academia repeatedly blocked me from doing so.

Anyone who has visited "10 different websites" pertaining to the CTMU and still "can't make heads or tails" of it is not trying hard enough to understand it. In the last several decades, I have heard similar complaints too many times to count. For what it's worth, essentially the same "unintelligibility" complaints were often heard about relativity theory and quantum mechanics (both of which are naturally embedded in the CTMU); it took many decades for this to change. But in the end, they prevailed. This is not only because they are good theories, but because they were introduced by professional academics, and were therefore taken seriously in Academia. Otherwise, they would have had no chance whatsoever.

Instead of railing against the CTMU and its author, those who find this state of affairs untenable should demand a reasonable accounting of the global academic bureaucracy, which has fattened beyond measure on the claim that it dutifully seeks, preserves, and disseminates valuable knowledge regardless of its nature or its source. In light of my own very telling experiences, this claim is not merely unjustifiable, but false on its face.

Thanks for your interest in the CTMU!

June 3, 2017

TRUMP, DONALD

Intelligence

237. President Trump is now claiming to have one of the highest IQs. What would you estimate it to be?

With all due respect, I suggest that some of the respondents here try to suck it up a little and come to grips with reality. In fact, Donald Trump would very likely qualify for Mensa. There's plenty of evidence for this, not least his success as a negotiator and businessman. Even with his (appreciable) head start in life, he could not have expanded his holdings in the various directions he chose with a "double-digit IQ". One need not be a sublime genius to juggle all of the irons that he has in the fire, but one can't exactly be a chimpanzee either. In Trump's world, smart people are always trying to take advantage of you and come out on top. You can't defend yourself from them without meeting a certain threshold of intellectual ability.

Ever hear of the "double-life strategy"? That's where a very intelligent person, realizing that he must communicate effectively with those around him in order to be successful (and avoid resentment and ostracism), adopts their verbal mannerisms and habits of expression so as to be accepted in their circles and smoothly interact with them. In New York (where I lived for over 25 years), that means Trump-style vernacular and plentiful hand gestures ... unless, of course, one has the luxury of existing in an isolated, privileged, snowflake-populated bubble-world of the kinds which proliferate in the academic, artistic, political, and corporate spheres.

Many people disagree with Mr. Trump's ideas and policy proposals on philosophical grounds. That's fine, as long as one does not confuse "philosophical grounds" with ad hominem attacks on his intelligence. Stop making yourselves look bad to people who actually have the brainpower to see through your emotional polemics. (Thanks.)

February 4, 2017

238. What is your honest estimation of Trump's IQ?

Trump's IQ is probably at least as high as that of the typical professional academic, and higher than that of the typical Harvard student.

When a sample of 86 Harvard undergraduates was given an abbreviated version of the WAIS, their mean IQ came up as 128.1, with a range of 97-148 (lower than would be estimated from the SAT scores of Harvard students, but the SAT is not an IQ test). The mean IQ of tenured college professors is probably around 135.

Anyone who thinks that Donald Trump couldn't easily work as a high-functioning professor at a top business school like the one from which he graduated (Wharton) hasn't been watching him very closely. Success of that magnitude doesn't lie, not even with four strategic bankruptcies (The Trump Taj Mahal, 1991; Trump Plaza Hotel, 1992; Trump Hotels and Casino Resorts, 2004; Trump Entertainment Resorts, 2009). Anyone who would walk down a university hallway and pass by a business management course taught by Trump in order to reach one taught by almost anyone else either has a bee in his bonnet, or rocks in his head.

One can disagree with Trump's politics and dislike his personal style all one likes, but his detractors need to stop fooling themselves about how sharp he is.

July 8, 2017

WIKIPEDIA

CTMU page

239. Is the current Wikipedia summary of the CTMU (available on the page for the author) a good summary of the theory?

Not really. The absence of a dedicated CTMU article on Wikipedia is a travesty that was engineered by some very aggressive yet very deceptive people circa 2006, and is quite possibly the worst show in Wikipedia history.

My involvement began when I was informed by a concerned party – whom I had never met – that two articles on Wikipedia were embroiled in controversy. One was a biography article about me; one was an article on my theory of mathematical metaphysics, the Cognitive Theoretic Model of the Universe (CTMU).

Apparently, some number of Wikipedia editors, administrators, and arbitrators had decided among themselves that neither I nor the CTMU – both of which had received considerable international publicity from, for example, ABC, NBC, and Popular Science (among other highly reputable sources) – were sufficiently notable for Wikipedia's elevated standards. In particular, they falsely but adamantly maintained that both articles had been created by me (they had not), were being jealously controlled by me despite alleged conflicts of interest (they were not), and that the CTMU was baseless and did not belong on Wikipedia (it is factual and logically verifiable, and even if it were not, it was still sufficiently notable to merit description). Both articles were nominated for deletion. (Another article on the Mega Foundation, a nonprofit 501.c.3 corporation in continuous operation since 1999, was created and deleted during this period.)

In the course of the ensuing proceedings, which can only be described as a witch hunt culminating in a kangaroo court, the CTMU was repeatedly misclassified as "Intelligent Design" when in fact, it predates and is independent of ID theory, and was snidely compared to nonsense like the "Time Cube" and other theoretical oddities often used as targets for the spitballs of those who fancy themselves "defenders of science". I finally traced the initial push to remove these articles to a website called "the brights.net", a pseudoskeptical anti-ID website run in keeping with the atheist-materialist convictions of such opinionated people as Richard Dawkins, Daniel Dennett, and James Randi. Unfortunately, this initiative – the true nature of which its promoters made every attempt to conceal – was immediately latched onto by a number of prominent Wikipedians, some of whom apparently still lurk behind the curtains to this very day.

Ultimately, the biography article was kept, but the CTMU article was deleted and the "earth was salted" against its recreation (a phrase I seem to recall being used by one or more of those clamoring for deletion). The experience left such a bad taste in my mouth that personally, I wouldn't care whether a CTMU article ever appears on Wikipedia were it not for others constantly using the platform to take credit for CTMU ideas without proper attribution. If experience be our guide, such an article would only be ruthlessly attacked and used as a platform for defamation and misattribution by certain nefarious parties still concealed in the Wikipedia woodwork. On the other hand, we might hope that Wikipedia is no longer such a nest of spiders, and that it is no longer controlled by sneaky little arachnids secretly communicating and coordinating with each other and using their mutual connections and experience in navigating the bureaucratic web to suppress those with whom they disagree.

In fairness to Wikipedia, which I and many others sometimes find very useful, a "peoples' encyclopedia" is by nature a very hard thing to run. Such a project naturally tends to be dominated by aggressive and opinionated people who operate largely behind the scenes, resulting in a "hive" whose inner mechanics are largely hidden as its drones and workers succumb to various forms of censorship and peer pressure and eventually veer away from sound encyclopedic principles of fairness, veracity, and scholarship.

Had I not ultimately appealed directly to the Head of the Wikimedia Foundation, Jimmy Wales (who evidently interceded even though I never received an official reply from him), there might be no mention of either me or the CTMU on Wikipedia to this day. In effect, we'd have been obliterated from the Internet "hive mind" by people whose motives may simply have been misguided, but whose tactics were inarguably as black and dirty as sin.

May 20, 2018

240. Why is there no Wikipedia page about the CTMU?

First, let me say that I think Wikipedia is a great idea, and I sometimes get some real use out of it. It has many fine and dedicated editors. But it also has its problems.

In particular, Wikipedia is notorious for its freewheeling bands of obsessive and seemingly jobless "vigilante trolls" who, after getting a bee in their bonnets about something they find annoying or offensive, stop at nothing to get it deleted. They usually begin by tampering with its article, pumping it full of defamation and misinformation; then, should someone else try to repair the damage, by complaining to administrators and nominating the article for deletion; and finally, when their case is heard, by engaging in nonstop lying and cheating while threatening any and all opponents with dire consequences until they get their way.

Then, after the article has been thoroughly nuked, they keep buzzing around the crater like flies around an outhouse to make sure it never comes back.

Some of these trolls are mere editors; some are administrators; in the past, some were arbitrators. They are overwhelmingly of a "secular" (atheist-materialist) persuasion; thus, if any of them encounters anything on the web which seems to suggest that a potential target mentions God, or spirituality ("woo"), or was written by a theist (particularly a Christian, AKA an "Intelligent Design Creationist"), that's usually the end of it. Whether or not what they've read about their target or victim is correct – and in the case of the CTMU, it was absolutely false – they immediately freak out *en masse* and throw a collective fit until the object of their displeasure has been red-inked, ripped out, and consigned to oblivion. They don't even bother to read the source material. The whole routine is approximately as sane and rational as a medieval witch hunt.

Unfortunately, I'm not exaggerating. The CTMU and I were attacked as being "non-notable" even after having been on every major news network in North America and Europe, with considerable mass media exposure in South America and Asia as well, and were insulted and harangued by self-styled Wikipedia "mathematicians" and "physicists" whose actual command of these disciplines couldn't have exceeded that of an average high schooler. It eventually emerged that the whole Wikipedia anti-CTMU movement had migrated from the website of "the Brights", a shrine to the dubious brand of "rationalism" promoted by various celebrity atheists who run around deploring "the supernatural" and claiming to love "science", but who often seem unable to distinguish worthwhile science, mathematics, and philosophy from soggy corn flakes.

Perhaps the CTMU article will come back some day. It certainly should, because the CTMU has nothing to do with "intelligent design", it has thousands of followers, it is backed up by several peer-reviewed publications, it has urgent social, scientific, and philosophical applications, and it is based on exciting new mathematics. The deletion of its article may have been Wikipedia's darkest day, and it should definitely be put right. But one thing is for sure: I'm not wasting any of my own time to make it happen.

September 20, 2018

SUBJECT INDEX

vs physical naturalism, 122
predicate logic, 123
properties of, 124
propositional logic, 125
self-justifying tautology, 125
structure of truth, 126, 127
tool for studying reality, 127

M

MASS MEDIA

indoctrination, 129

MATHEMATICS

on conceptual abstrac-
tions, 131
illogical exclusion, 131
on infinitesimals, 132
in natural sciences, 132
P vs NP problem, 133
problem solving, 134
proving God's existence, 135
pure mathematics, 135

MEGA FOUNDATION

operations, 137

METAPHYSICS

cosmology, 138
definition, 138
Dyson, Freeman, 139
epistemology and ontol-
ogy, 140
framework of reality, 141
metalogical system, 141
metaphysical metalan-
guage, 142
and philosophy, 142
and physics, 143
scope of, 143

MULTIPLEX UNITY

coherent interconnec-
tion, 145

MUSK, ELON

evaluating utility, 146
outlier or not, 147
productivity, 147

P

PETERSON, JORDAN

debate invitation, 151
worldview assessment, 151

PHILOSOPHY

arrogation by Academia, 153
Cartesian mind-body dual-
ism, 154
Chris Langan and Immanuel
Kant, 155
Harris, Sam, 155
Hume, David, 156
of physics, 156
prevalence of physical-
ism, 156

PHYSICS

force of gravity, 159
Hawking, Stephen, 159
indispensability of logic, 160
particles in CTMU, 161
physicists and CTMU, 161
Wheeler, John, 162

POLITICS

gun control, 163, 164
identity politics, 165

Made in United States
North Haven, CT
14 December 2024

62515289R00134